ROUTLEDGE LIBRARY EDITIONS:
19TH CENTURY RELIGION

Volume 6

RELIGION

RELIGION

LEONARD W. COWIE

Routledge
Taylor & Francis Group
LONDON AND NEW YORK

First published in 1973 by Methuen Educational Ltd

This edition first published in 2018
by Routledge
2 Park Square, Milton Park, Abingdon, Oxon OX14 4RN

and by Routledge
711 Third Avenue, New York, NY 10017

Routledge is an imprint of the Taylor & Francis Group, an informa business

British Library Cataloguing in Publication Data
A catalogue record for this book is available from the British Library

ISBN: 978-1-138-06800-1 (Set)
ISBN: 978-1-315-10089-0 (Set) (ebk)
ISBN: 978-1-138-08431-5 (Volume 6) (hbk)
ISBN: 978-1-138-08434-6 (Volume 6) (pbk)
ISBN: 978-1-315-11185-8 (Volume 6) (ebk)

Publisher's Note
The publisher has gone to great lengths to ensure the quality of this reprint but points out that some imperfections in the original copies may be apparent.

Religion

Leonard W. Cowie

METHUEN EDUCATIONAL
London · Toronto · Sydney · Wellington

First published 1973
by Methuen Educational Ltd
11 New Fetter Lane, London EC4P 4EE

Filmset in Photon Times 11 on 13 pt. by
Richard Clay (The Chaucer Press), Ltd, Bungay, Suffolk
and printed in Great Britain by
Fletcher & Son Ltd, Norwich

SBN 423 44850 1 HB
423 44860 9 PB

Contents

Acknowledgements

Permission to reproduce illustrations is gratefully acknowledged to the Church Missionary Society for pages 16, 118, 125 and 128; the University Church of St Mary the Virgin, Oxford, for page 37; John Murray (reproduced from D. C. Lathbury, *Letters on Church and Religion of William Ewart Gladstone*, 2 vols, 1910) for page 52 (both); Malcolm Powell, East Grinstead, for page 63; the National Portrait Gallery for pages 99 and 132.

Preface

‘No one will ever understand Victorian England who does not appreciate that among highly civilized, in contradistinction to more primitive, countries it was one of the most religious that the world has known,’ wrote Sir Robert Ensor in *England 1870–1914* (Oxford History of England, vol. xiv). This book offers a contribution towards this important aspect of nineteenth-century England, taking the nineteenth century to cover the period from 1815 to 1914. It is based upon a selection of extracts from contemporary documents illustrating the development of religious groups and movements. These extracts are linked by a text which seeks to provide a background which will enable the reader to study them further himself and assess their meaning and importance.

No book on this subject could hope to be comprehensive, and one of this size is bound to omit a number of important questions, particularly the influence of religion upon such topics as politics, science, education and morality. As many as possible of these, however, will be included within the scope of other volumes in this series.

The range of documentary material available for a book of this sort is extensive. Parliament concerned itself on several occasions with important legislation on ecclesiastical matters, and the law courts were called upon to hear cases concerning them. Bishops and other denominational leaders made pronouncements and issued manifestos which were reported fully in the daily newspapers. There was also a flourishing religious press which published weighty articles and readers’ letters. It was an age of great preachers, and sermons were not only heard by large congregations, but also bought widely when published. Finally, lengthy biographies of the ‘life and letters’ type were written of all the important figures of the time (and of some who were not so important as well).

In selecting from this wealth of contemporary evidence, an attempt has been made to achieve as great a diversity as possible and to use examples which, while relevant and appropriate, draw upon all the varieties of material. In addition, while some comparatively well-known evidence has had to be used, less familiar extracts have been included where these are available to illustrate the subject. And in using the extracts, reference has been given to their inclusion in collections of documents and other similar sources where the originals are not likely to be readily available.

The attitude towards religious history and, therefore, the interpretation of its material, has changed within comparatively recent years. In the past, denominational histories, such as the *History of the English Church*, edited by W. Hunt and W. R. W. Stephens, which appeared in nine volumes in the early years of this century, predominated. These were modelled upon the ordinary general histories of the time which regarded politics and constitutional development as the proper scope of historical writing. Nowadays, corresponding to the wider horizon of historians in other fields, the changed attitude of ecclesiastical historians may be seen in such pioneer books as Bernard Manning, *The People's Faith in the Time of Wyclif* (1919), and H. Maynard Smith, *Pre-Reformation England* (1938), or, dealing with the nineteenth century, the chapter entitled 'The Religion of the People' in G. Kitson Clark, *The Making of Victorian England* (1962), or E. R. Wickham, *Church and People in an Industrial City* (1957), which is a local study of the various religious bodies in Sheffield.

Such an approach by the reader of the documents in this book does, however, take him into a field of history that may be unknown territory for him. It was an age very different from our own, an age when W. E. Gladstone wrote a book in defence of the literal interpretation of the Bible (*The Impregnable Rock of Holy Scripture*, (1890)) and scorned those who only went to church once on Sundays, and an age when three successive Lord Chancellors taught in Sunday Schools throughout their careers. It was an age also of religious contention and strife, when churchmen and Nonconformists would boast that they had never entered each other's places of worship, an age in which the origins of the modern ecumenical movement seem very difficult to trace. It was an age too when religion was an everyday topic of conversation, and its beliefs and traditions were understood as they are not today; and hence the *glossary* at the end of this book to explain some of the words and phrases used in the documents. The reader must, therefore, come to this subject with an awareness of its attitude towards religion and an appreciation of its character along the lines suggested in the text of this book.

This book also indicates the circumstances in which these documents came into being, and this factor must govern the critical approach of the reader towards them. Each of them appeared at the time for a definite, contemporary purpose, perhaps polemical, devotional, judicial or hortative, and he must, of course, bear this in mind and come to his own conclusions as to their meaning and value. This book gives him some guidance about this, but does not attempt to do it for him.

Nor does this book attempt a verdict upon the religious history of the period as a whole. It may seem to end, as the twentieth century got under way, upon a negative note of uncertainty, but the people themselves of those pre-1914 times realized that the future was far from certain, and the prophets who sought to divine the future of religion had good grounds for speaking without assurance. The meaning of this period and its relation to the equally uncertain present pose questions which the reader of this book must consider himself.

(N.B.: terms explained in the Glossary are indicated in the text by an asterisk.)

1 Introduction

The nineteenth century was a strongly religious age in England. As on the Continent, there was a revival of religion in the years after 1815 which gave the century its fundamental aspect. Nevertheless, the opening years of the period hardly suggested that the English people as a whole were likely to become religious. Christianity was established in the form of the Church of England, but about a quarter of the people were Nonconformists, estranged from the Church of England and often bitterly hostile to it, while the Church itself was crippled by serious weaknesses and abuses. The Church of England was bound to be of key importance in any religious revival. Its recovery was essential, and yet the situation was confused and uncertain and seemed to have been made yet more so by the effects in England of the French Revolution.

The outbreak of the French Revolution, though at first hailed with joy by some in England, soon aroused dread and dismay among the upper, governing classes. The most influential denunciation of the revolutionaries was Edmund Burke's *Reflections on the Revolution in France*, published in 1790. To him the Revolution was a threat, not only to political stability and public order, but also to the place of the Christian religion in society. He appealed to the tradition, rooted in Medieval Christendom, which regarded Church and State as an inseparable, united entity, settled and sanctioned in the law of England:

> The English people do not consider their church establishment as convenient, but as essential to their state; not as a thing heterogeneous and separable; something added for accommodation; that they may either keep or lay aside, according to their temporary ideas of convenience. They consider it as the foundation of their whole constitution, with which, and with every part of which, it holds an indissoluble union. Church and state are ideas inseparable in their minds, and scarcely is the one ever mentioned without mentioning the other.
>
> Edmund Burke, *Reflections on the Revolution in France* (1852 ed.), 80.

This conception was still held by many churchmen, and it was to be given fresh expression by the first Tractarians; but it was entirely unacceptable to the

Nonconformist bodies, who not only opposed the Church of England on matters of faith and organization, but also resented the privileges which they considered it enjoyed unfairly through its established position. They now largely had freedom in the exercise of their religion, but were subject to a number of objectionable restrictions on their activities as citizens. Though the seventeenth-century Test and Corporation Acts,* designed to exclude them from governmental and administrative office, had ceased to affect them in practice, they were excluded from Oxford and Cambridge, had to pay Church Rates* and could not use their own marriage and burial services. Joseph Priestley, the theologian and scientist, expressed the Nonconformist outlook in a reply to Burke:

> The *church of Christ* is built upon a rock, and we are assured that *the gates of hell shall not prevail against it.* Now, had this church of yours, whose fears and cries have always been the signal of alarm to all its neighbours, been made of proper materials, and constructed in a proper manner, had it been built upon this rock of *truth*, it would never have had anything to fear . . . Should the *state* itself be overturned, the people would, of themselves, and from predilection, reinstate their favourite *church* in all its former rights and privileges. But you are sensible it has not this hold on the minds of the people, and you justly suspect, that, if any misfortune should happen to it, they would never rebuild it, but, if left to their own free choice, would adopt some other plan, more useful and commodious.
>
> Joseph Priestley, *Letters to Burke* (1791), 113–14.

It seemed, therefore, that there was very serious opposition to the revival of the idea of the Church of England as a national Church. Nor was this only because of the expressed opposition of the Nonconformists. History had deprived the Church of England of popular support in both country and town. In the countryside it had long been associated with the squires and the wealthy farmers, and the clergy identified themselves with this class and accepted the deep-rooted contemporary social order. Joseph Arch, later to be the pioneer of trade unionism among the agricultural labourers, recalled how this was so during the 1830s in the Warwickshire village of Barford where he spent his childhood. His father was an agricultural labourer, and the practice which Joseph Arch described was fairly common in rural churches at this time. In some villages the communion of those who went up to the altar first was called the 'First Table' and of those who followed the 'Second Table'. Anyone bold enough to go up before those of the rest of his class would have to face general disapproval:

> I never took the Communion in my parish church in my life. When I was

seven years old I saw something which prevented me once for all. One Sunday my father was going to stop to take the Communion, and I, being a boy, had of course to go out before it began. I may here mention that the church opened then in a direct line with the chancel and the main aisle, so that anyone looking through the keyhole could easily see what was going on inside. The door is now to the side of the church and out of direct line with the chancel. I was a little bit of a fellow and curious. I said to myself, 'What does father stop behind for? What is it they do? I'll see.' So I went out of the church, closed the door, placed my eye at the keyhole and peeped through, and what I saw will be engraved on my mind until the last day of my life. That sight caused a wound which has never been healed. My proud little spirit smarted and burned when I saw what happened at the Communion service.

First up walked the squire to the communion rails; the farmers went up next; then up went the tradesmen, the shopkeepers, the wheelwright and the blacksmith; and then, the very last of all, went the poor agricultural labourers in their smock frocks. They walked up by themselves; nobody else knelt with them; it was as if they were unclean—and at that sight the iron entered straight into my poor little heart and remained fast embedded there. I said to myself, 'If that's what goes on—never for me!' I ran home and told my mother what I had seen, and I wanted to know why my father was not as good in the eyes of God as the squire, and why the poor should be forced to come up last of all to the table of the Lord. My mother gloried in my spirit.

Joseph Arch, *The Story of his Life Told by Himself* (ed. Frances, Countess of Warwick, 2nd ed., 1898), 19–20.

In the towns and especially in the new industrial areas, Methodism was firmly rooted. John Wesley had thought of his movement as seeking 'to reform the nation, more particularly the Church, and to spread Scriptural holiness over the land'. It developed into a popular Christianity such as had never been known in England, at any rate since the Middle Ages. He had not intended that his followers should leave the Church of England, but his ways were not those of the established religion, and formal separation came soon after his death in 1791. By 1815 there were some 200,000 Methodists in England, most of whom were to be found among the lower classes and (although village preaching was now gaining adherents in the countryside) mostly in the urban areas. Here they had established themselves where the Church had failed to evangelize successfully and had provided religious care for thousands who had not known it before. In most large towns their chapels outnumbered the parish churches, and their worshippers were more numerous. Their religious outlook and practices often became accepted by the people in these places as the recognized expression of religion and exercised an influence even on the Anglican clergy.

In 1837, W. F. Hook went to be Vicar of Leeds, then a busy town of 88,000 people, mostly engaged in the woollen industry. After he had been there for four months, he depicted in a letter the religious situation as he found it there and the general reaction to his determination to establish the services of the parish church according to the principles which Tractarianism was now spreading among the clergy:

> As to religion, the traditional or established religion in Leeds is Methodism; and consequently, as is natural, since we breathe a Methodistic atmosphere, everything has a Methodistic tendency. A pious Churchman here means a person who likes an establishment and consequently supports the Church; but then the Church is not sufficient to supply his wants; so that he probably institutes two or three prayer-meetings in some large house or warehouse, where he can indulge in extemporaneous prayer and Methodistic rant. Nor do the people venture to entertain a notion that the Church is *right*; their mode of defence is to show that it is not so *very wrong* that it is sinful to belong to it; they *do* therefore belong to it, looking forward to the day when it will be reformed, i.e. brought down to the state of some Methodistic sect. Even many of the clergy, without knowing it, shape their doctrines and style of preaching according to the Methodistic system; and those who are not humdrum, labour not to instruct, but to excite. Then I have, to meet all this, a dirty, ugly hole of a church, in which it is impossible to perform divine service properly; the chancel, for example, being formed into an almost distinct church, and the body of the church being arranged to look as near as possible like a conventicle; which same ugly old church is located in the very St Giles's of Leeds. I am now preparing a plan for pulling the church half down and rebuilding it; but this will cost between three and four thousand pounds, and I fear to start the subscription now while trade is so bad. I am starting up the clergy by insisting upon the strictest rubrical observance in all the occasional services—baptisms, marriages and funerals. Nobody here seems to have a noting that baptism is anything more than a form of registration; I think it is my duty therefore to have it always administered with peculiar solemnity. They do stare sometimes when I tell them that before administering the Sacrament, I require them to attend the prayers of the Church and pray with me: they think by the Sacrament I must needs mean the Lord's Supper.
>
> W. R. W. Stephens, *The Life and Letters of Walter Farquhar Hook* (2 vols, 1879), I, 408–9.

Anglican reform as represented by Hook was, however, only slowly manifesting itself in 1815. On the whole, the Church seemed to be showing little capacity to adapt itself to meet the problems and challenges of the new century. It was conservative in outlook and hostile or indifferent to ideas of change or initiative. The rational, sceptical intellectual atmosphere of the eighteenth century had had a deadening influence upon it. It had become a Church in which 'enthusiasm' was equated with fanaticism or bigotry and greater importance was attached to ethical and moral precepts than to matters of belief or worship.

In fact, the French Revolution, which in England strengthened the ties between Church and State, at first delayed the coming of reform. Churchmen feared that the ideas of the Revolution were dangerously hostile to the Christian religion and its institutions. Tom Paine, who wrote *The Rights of Man* in 1791 in answer to Burke's *Reflections*, was an avowed republican and was widely regarded as an infamous infidel. Bishops and divines insisted in their sermons upon the inevitable connection of democratic principles and foreign subversion with irreligion and blasphemy. To cling to the existing order in Church and State seemed to them to be the only way of preserving the religion they were bound to defend.

The outlook of the Church of England at this time has been well expressed by J. A. Froude, the historian, whose father, as Archdeacon of Totnes in the years after the Napoleonic War, was typical among the clergy in upholding the Church 'as part of the constitution' and respecting the bishops as national authorities:

> The French Revolution had frightened all classes out of advanced ways of thinking, and society in town and country was Tory in politics and determined to allow no innovations upon the inherited faith. It was orthodox without being theological. Doctrinal problems were little thought of. Religion, as taught in the Church of England, meant moral obedience to the will of God. The speculative part of it was accepted because it was assumed to be true. The creeds were reverentially repeated; but the essential thing was practice. People went to church on Sunday to learn to be good, to hear the commandments repeated to them for the thousandth time and to see them written in gilt letters over the communion-table. About the power of the keys, the real presence or the metaphysics of doctrine, no one was anxious, for no one thought about them. It was not worth while to waste time on questions which had no bearing on conduct and could be satisfactorily disposed of only by sensible indifference.

J. A. Froude, *Short Studies on Great Subjects* (4 vols, 1886), IV, 239f.

Such a spirit of conservatism and fear of innovation ignored the vital need for reform in the Church. The English Reformation of the sixteenth century had changed its doctrine and worship, but left its weaknesses of organization unrelieved. Many medieval abuses were still prevalent. One third of the clergy were pluralists;* even more of them were non-resident.* Sometimes parishes were completely without a resident clergyman, the duties of the absent incumbent being performed by the neighbouring clergy or by a curate who came into the parish to take the services. Other such parishes were served by a resident curate, but he might receive only a pittance by way of payment from the incumbent whose job he was doing. There were mitigating circumstances on the side of absenteeism and pluralism. The endowment of the parishes was very uneven. Sometimes it was so small that an incumbent had to hold more than one parish in order to have an income on which he could live. Again, there were no clerical pensions or provision for illness, so that an aged or sick incumbent could only pay someone else to do his duty. Yet, the fact remained that most of the pluralists were not poor—their combined parishes were good ones and brought them very ample incomes; and most of the non-resident clergy were not incapacitated—they merely preferred to live in more pleasant parts of the country or even on the Continent.

The memories of S. Baring Gould, who was born in 1834 and spent his boyhood in Devonshire, describe vividly what these abuses could mean, especially in the more remote parts of the country, where change was slow:

> The parish of Lydford, the largest in England, comprising 50,751 acres—mostly indeed Dartmoor, but yet with Princetown in numbering a considerable population, and Lydford itself, distant from Princetown nearly fifteen miles by road, was held for a great many years by the Revd Dr Fletcher. This Fletcher was also Rector of Southill in Cornwall, one of the richest livings in the county, worth £594 per annum—twenty-five miles from Lydford, he held this with the church and rectory situated three miles from the town of Callington, also in the parish. For many years I knew the successive curates of Lydford, but never heard of Dr Fletcher visiting the place to take duty in it. The chancel roof was in holes, and on one Christmas Day the holy table was spread with a covering of snow. In my own parish, the Rector, Mr Elford, was non-resident. He lived nine miles off, at Tavistock. When the Bishop demurred to this, 'How can I live,' said he, 'in a place where there is no barber to trim my wig?' And this was accepted as sufficient excuse. From 1795 to 1811 Elford held as well the curacy of Coryton, under the Revd R. V. Willesford, who was a pluralist Rector. This man was also

Vicar of Brentnor, Vicar of Awelscombe, near Honiton, Curate of Tavistock and Headmaster of Tavistock Grammar School from 1795 to 1821.

S. Baring Gould, *Church Revival* (1914), 127–18.

The main reason for these abuses in the Church was that it still possessed no central administrative body. Queen Anne's Bounty distributed to the poorest parishes certain crown revenues, which had originally been diverted from the Church at the Reformation and were restored by Queen Anne, but there was no other way of making any redistribution of the Church's income. Since the early eighteenth century, the Convocations of Canterbury and York, the ancient assemblies of the clergy, had been forbidden to transact business. Even the creation of a new parish required a separate Act of Parliament. The outward signs of such a situation were to be seen not only in the parishes, but in the cathedrals and great town churches as well. Anthony Trollope wrote in *The Warden* of the impression made upon the Revd Septimus Harding when, during his brief visit to London, he attended Matins at Westminster Abbey:

> The minor canon* hurried in, somewhat late, in a surplice not in the neatest order, and was followed by a dozen choristers, who were also not as trim as they might have been: they all jostled into their places with a quick hurried step, and the service was soon commenced. Soon commenced and soon over, for there was no music, and time was not unnecessarily lost in the chanting.

Anthony Trollope, *The Warden* (Penguin ed, 1944), 135.

In such circumstances, it was only to be expected that the Church was unpopular among many classes of people and that the clergy should be regarded with widespread contempt or hostility. By 1815 the movement known as the Industrial Revolution had become well established in England, with its far-reaching economic and social consequences which had largely taken the government, the employers and the country as a whole by surprise. The problems of town life, the conditions of factory employment and the needs of a new working-class placed an unprecedented strain upon the old machinery of government and the motives of those who administered it. By their position in society the clergy were generally inclined to take a very limited view of the situation. Most were concerned with the threat it posed to law and order and did not possess sufficient knowledge or imagination to comprehend the circumstances of the masses.

Of course, it is possible to exaggerate. There were those among the clergy who felt for the circumstances of the poor and were ready to do what they could to relieve their sufferings, even if they could not comprehend any means of social reform to remove the causes of their distress. William Cobbett, who was not well disposed towards the clergy generally and towards bishops in particular, recounted an incident which showed Charles Richard Sumner, Bishop of Winchester from 1827 to 1869, at least to be possessed of an ability to be brought to understand the plight of others:

> I have at last found a Bishop of the *Law* Church to *Praise.* The facts are these: the Bishop (Sumner), in coming from Winchester to his palace at Farnham, was met about a mile before he got to the latter place, by a band of sturdy beggars, whom some call robbers. They stopped his carriage and asked for some money, which he gave them. But he did not *prosecute* them: he had not a man of them called to account for his conduct, but, the next day, set *twenty-four labourers to constant work*, opened his Castle to the distressed of all ages, and supplied all with food and other necessaries who stood in need of them. This was becoming a Christian teacher.
>
> William Cobbett, *Political Register*, 15th January 1831. Quoted J. H. & Barbara Hammond, *The Village Labourer* (3rd ed, 1920), 240.

Again, there were those among the parish clergy who performed their duties conscientiously and cared for their flock. George Eliot in *Adam Bede* characterized such a clergyman in the person of the Revd Adolphus Irwine, who was a threefold pluralist and yet:

> Although he would probably have declined to give his body to be burned in any public cause, and was far from bestowing all his goods to feed the poor, he had that charity which has sometimes been lacking to very illustrious virtue—he was tender to other men's failings and unwilling to impute evil. He was one of those men, and they are not the commonest, of whom we can know the best only by following them away from the market-place, the platform and the pulpit, entering with them into their own homes, hearing the voice with which they speak to the young and aged about their own hearth-stone, and witnessing their thoughtful care for the everyday wants of everyday companions, who take all their kindness as a matter of course and not as a subject for panegyric. Such men, happily, have lived in times when great abuses have flourished and have sometimes even been living representatives of the abuses.
>
> George Eliot, *Adam Bede* (1905), 52.

Life was not easy for many of the clergy. They had little assistance or supervision in their task, and the country clergy had often to face an oppressive isolation, physical and spiritual. Thomas Mozley, who came to know the incumbents of the villages on

Salisbury Plain in the 1830s and 1840s, appreciated their circumstances and came to admire the way in which they endured them:

> They were all men of learning, of mental gifts, of good intentions, and of sound principles, though with their differences, and some with their deficiencies. As regards the great centres of religious or literary circulation, it was in every case something of a banishment. I honestly believe that there was not one of the Christian Fathers of the first three centuries who would not have held it a living martyrdom to be consigned to such banishment, amid barbarians and other cattle. They all did their duty, though encountering many difficulties, and frequently meeting with little encouragement. With all of them their duty was really quite optional, but they all worked for God, and not for man.
>
> T. Mozley, *Reminiscences Chiefly of Towns, Villages and Schools* (2 vols, 1885), I, 348.

Over the religious situation throughout the country in 1815, therefore, there hung a great question mark. The Church of England was largely somnolent. The older Nonconformist bodies shared in that somnolence. The Methodist movement was the spearhead of a revival which had already begun and had already gained for itself thousands of adherents; but after its founder's death its future was unsure, and divisions had appeared among its members. Yet the French Revolution, which at first had seemed to add to the confusion of the situation, was to do much to establish for religion a sure place in the life of the country during the century. All had not been lost, and among both clergy and people there were those ready to face the issues of the time.

2 The Evangelicals

The party within the Church of England which seemed in 1815 to offer the greatest promise of inspiring a religious revival was that of the Evangelicals. They had owed some of their inspiration to Wesley; but they essentially formed an independent movement and differed from the Methodists in doctrine and in the acceptance of the system of the Church. They did, however, share with Wesley the same insistence upon the need for personal conversion and acceptance of Christ; and this not infrequently drew upon them the same prejudice and opposition.

This happened later in the country districts than in the towns, as witness the experiences of Henry Moule, father of a future Bishop of Durham and an earnest Evangelical, who became Vicar of Fordington in Dorset in 1829:

> Great contempt for religion was common in Fordington. And when the new vicar was found to be the preacher of a gospel of definite and personal change of heart and consequent devotion of life, he had much to bear in the way of opposition and even of personal insult. Careless groups at the churchyard gates reviled the worshippers as they went in. Nor was the other side of society much more favourable. At a meet of the hounds, Mr Moule was discussed and pronounced to be a 'Methodist'; as such he was a person to whom courtesies were scarcely due.

J. H. Harford & F. C. MacDonald, *Bishop Handley Moule* (1922), 3.

It was in their preaching that the Evangelicals were most commonly pronounced to be 'Methodistical'; and, like the Methodists, the Evangelicals believed firmly in the power of fervent preaching. The eighteenth-century clergy had read their formal sermons with a minimum of gestures; to do otherwise would have been a sign of 'enthusiasm'. The difference the Evangelicals made can be seen from remarks by John Newton, the converted slave-trader, about the sermons of one of the first of the Evangelicals, William Grimshaw, who was Vicar of Haworth in Yorkshire from 1742 to 1763. Newton was writing in 1799 and recalling a visit he had made to Haworth nearly forty years before:

The desire of usefulness to persons of the weakest capacity, or most destitute of the advantages of education, influenced his phraseology in preaching. Though his abilities as a preacher, and his fund of knowledge, rendered him very competent to stand before great men; yet as his stated hearers were mostly of the poorer and unlettered class, he condescended to accommodate himself, in the most familiar manner, to their ideas and their mode of expression. Like the Apostle, he disdained the elegance and excellence of speech which is admired of those that seek entertainment perhaps not less than instruction from the pulpit; he chose rather to deliver his message in what he used to term *market language*; and though the warmth of his heart, and the rapidity of his imagination might sometimes lead him to clothe his thoughts in words which even a candid critic could not wholly justify, yet the general effect of his 'plain' manner was striking and impressive, suited to make the dullest understand, and to fix for the time the attention of the most careless. Frequently a sentence, which a delicate hearer might judge quaint or vulgar, conveyed an important truth to the ear and fixed it in the memory years after the rest of the sermon had been forgotten. Judicious hearers could easily excuse some escapes of this kind and allow that, though he had a singular felicity in bringing down the great truths of the Gospel to the level of the meanest capacity, he did not degrade them. The solemnity of his manner, the energy with which he spoke, the spirit of love that beamed in his eyes and breathed through his addresses were convincing proofs that he did not trifle with his people. I may give my judgement upon this point, something in his own way, by quoting a plain and homely proverb which says *that it is the best cat which catches the most mice.* His improprieties, if he was justly charged with any, are easily avoided, but very few ministers have had equal success. But if his language was more especially suited to the taste of his unpolished rustic hearers, his subject matter was calculated to affect the hearts of all, whether high or low, rich or poor, learned or ignorant; and they who refused were compelled to tremble.

John Newton, *Memoirs of the Life of William Grimshaw* (1799), 126.

Another contribution to worship which the Evangelicals shared with the Methodists was the writing of hymns and their use by congregations. Probably the most notable Evangelical hymn-writer was Augustus Montague Toplady, who was Vicar of Broad Hembury in Devonshire and published his well-known 'Rock of Ages' in 1775. The Evangelicals were Calvinists in doctrine, and this hymn expresses their belief in the utter sinfulness of man and his complete inability to achieve his own salvation:

Not the labours of my hands
Can fulfil thy law's demands;
Could my zeal no respite know,
Could my tears for ever flow,
All for sin could not atone:
Thou must save, and thou alone.

Songs of Praise, no. 636.

In 1815 the most prominent Evangelical figure was Charles Simeon, who was Vicar of Holy Trinity Church, Cambridge, from 1783 until his death in 1836. At first his church was made the scene of disgraceful riotings, but he was unafraid in the face of either ridicule or persecution, and his single-minded, consistent efforts won him converts. Situated in a university centre, his possibilities were great, and he used them to the best of his ability. His influence spread, through his religious character and habit, his sermons and, abcve all in the University, his weekly parties on Friday evenings for undergraduates, to which sometimes as many as forty came. In 1829 he answered an inquiry by a clergyman at Oxford about these parties:

> My own habit is this: I have an open day, when all who choose it come to take their tea with me. Everyone is at liberty to ask what questions he will, and I give to them the best answer I can. Hence a great variety of subjects come under review—subjects which we could not discuss in the pulpit—and the young men find it a very edifying season. We have neither exposition, as such, nor prayer; but I have opportunity of saying all that my heart can wish, without the formality of a set ordinance . . . You need not expound; but if there be any passage of Scripture, which you think of peculiar importance for their consideration, you may easily, without being a conjurer, contrive to have their attention turned to it; and you can easily recommend the young men to pray over it in secret.
>
> W. Carus, *Memoirs of the Life of the Revd Charles Simeon* (1847), 641.

From Cambridge went a steady stream of young men who became ordained and sought to put into practice all over the country the Evangelical principles they had learnt from Simeon; but he observed with sorrow that a squire or other patron might appoint, in succession to an Evangelical incumbent, an idle or fox-hunting parson. He therefore established in 1817 the Simeon Trust to which he contributed his wealth and large sums he solicited from sympathizers so that it might buy the patronage of parishes and appoint a succession of Evangelical clergymen to them. They must, he insisted, be good, conscientious men, but they must also be Evangelicals. Writing in 1823 of a legacy he had received some years earlier, he said:

I have for these many years determined to devote a great part of the principal, and all the interest, to the service of our Common Lord, who gave His own life a ransom for us. The object I have selected and prosecuted for several years has been the purchase of Livings (which I commit to Trustees in perpetuity) that in them may be preached those doctrines which have produced so happy an effect on my own soul.

C. J. Morton (ed), *Charles Simeon, An Interpretation* (1936), 94–5.

Unlike Methodism, Evangelicalism was strongest among the upper and middle classes, who had never completely lost touch with the Church and who had been brought to an increased seriousness of life and demeanour as a result of the French Revolution. The old, fashionable indifference to morals became a thing of the past with them. They were increasingly ready to listen to the message of Evangelicalism, and through them the Evangelicals were able, in their turn, to exercise a profound effect upon the life of the country.

Indeed, an important strength of Evangelicalism was the number of wealthy and influential laymen who were attracted to it. The most important of these belonged to an informal group nicknamed by Sydney Smith, the witty Canon* of St Paul's, the 'Clapham Sect', because they lived near Clapham, then a fashionable village just outside London, and worshipped at the parish church under John Venn, its Evangelical Rector. They included William Wilberforce, a member of a prominent commercial family in Hull; Zachary Macaulay, a retired colonial governor; Lord Teignmouth, a retired Indian administrator; Charles Grant, Chairman of the East India Company; and James Stephen, a prominent Member of Parliament. When the latter's son wrote about the group, Zachary Macaulay's son, the future Lord Macaulay, commented to his sister in 1844:

I think Stephen's article on the Clapham Sect the best thing he ever did. I do not think with you that the Claphamites were men too obscure for such delineation. The truth is that from that little knot of men emanated all the Bible Societies and almost all the Missionary societies in the world. The whole organisation of the Evangelical party was their work. The share which they had in providing means for the education of the people was great. They were really the destroyers of the slave-trade and of slavery. Many of those whom Stephen describes were public men of the greatest weight. Lord Teignmouth governed India at Calcutta. Grant governed India in Leadenhall Street. Stephen's father was Perceval's right-hand man in the House of Commons. It is needless to speak of Wilberforce. As to Simeon, if you knew what his authority and influence were, and how they extended from Cambridge to the most remote corners of England, you would allow that his real sway in the Church was far greater than that of any primate.

Sir George Otto Trevelyan, *Life and Letters of Lord Macaulay* (1890), 49–50.

The best known of these Evangelicals at Clapham was undoubtedly William Wilberforce. Born in 1759 into the wealth gained by successful trade, he was educated at Cambridge and was elected to Parliament in 1780. During a tour of the Continent in 1784–5 with an Evangelical divine, Isaac Milner, he was aroused to an interest in religion, and reading the New Testament led him further to conversion to Evangelicalism. At first he wished to seek ordination, but he was dissuaded from this by John Newton, who urged him to serve the cause of Christianity by using his position in society and Parliament. This he henceforward did, showing a genuinely pastoral concern for the eternal welfare of his friends and putting at risk his close friendship with the Younger Pitt by trying to secure his conversion. The earnestness of his efforts may be seen from a little document he compiled entitled 'Friends' Paper. To be Looked at every Sunday'. Its entries included:

S—— and Mrs. What books reading? To give them good ones—Walker's Sermons. Call on Mrs S. and talk a little. Lend her Venn's last Sermon. Education of their children to enquire about. Prayer, etc. Their coming some Sunday to Battersea Rise to hear Venn. Call often, and be kind.

Lady A—— and Sir R. Has he read Dodderidge? Be open to her, etc.

Mr and Mrs M——. Encourage to family prayers, etc.

Lord and Lady J——. See them. Get at them through G. Discover what books reading.

V——. Try what he believes and speak home truths.

The J——s. Call and sound them on religion. Give them money to give away, etc. Little presents.

Lady E——. Speak pretty openly, yet tenderly.

R. Coupland, *William Wilberforce* (1945), 236.

Soon he came into contact with the group of men, mainly Evangelicals, who were striving to obtain the abolition of the slave-trade and slavery, and he devoted the rest of his career as a Member of Parliament to the cause. The slave-trade was abolished in 1807 and slavery throughout the British Empire in 1833, the bill passing Parliament a few weeks after the death of Wilberforce, who had died, however, in the knowledge that it was already assured. As early as 1789 he had made a speech in the House of Commons in which he expressed the motives of himself and the anti-slavery movement during those years:

> So much misery condensed in so little room is more than the human imagination had ever before conceived. So enormous, so dreadful, so irremediable did its wickedness appear that my own mind was completely made up for the abolition. It is true indeed that my mind was harassed beyond measure. For when West India planters and merchants retorted it on me that it was the British Parliament had authorised this trade—when they said to me, 'It is your Acts of Parliament, it is your encouragement, it is faith in your laws, in your protection, that has tempted us into this trade, and has now made it necessary to us,' it was difficult to find an answer . . . I could not believe that the same Being, who forbids rapine and bloodshed, had made rapine and bloodshed necessary to the welfare of any part of His universe. I felt a confidence in this principle. I took the resolution to act upon it. And soon the light broke in upon me. The evidence I have to offer on this point is now decisive and complete. And I wish to observe—with submission, but with perfect conviction of heart—what an instance this is of how safely we may trust the rules of justice, the dictates of conscience, and the laws of God in opposition to the seeming impolicy of these eternal principles.
>
> S. C. Carpenter, *Church and People 1789–1889* (1933), 31.

The evils of slavery and the slave-trade had an important part in arousing the concern of the Evangelicals for overseas missionary work. The two existing societies of the Church, the Society for Promoting Christian Knowledge and the Society for the Propagation of the Gospel, both of which had been founded in the late seventeenth century, confined their efforts to North America and the West Indies, while the East India Company was not favourable towards missionary undertakings in its territory; but the Evangelicals felt keenly the need to make redress to Africa for the slave-trade. In 1806, the year before it was abolished, John Venn said:

> The Church of God in every country will turn their eyes from the desolations and vices, which now deform the earth, to the rising hope of better times, when the true knowledge of God will more generally prevail. They will look to the infant Church of Africa and will watch with anxious desire its progress. Africa expects from you some reparation for her wrongs.
>
> M. Hennell, *John Venn and the Clapham Sect* (1958), 244.

John Venn was in the chair at a meeting of twenty-five Evangelicals, held at the Castle and Falcon Inn in Aldersgate Street on 12th April 1799, to consider the question of founding 'in the Established Church a society for sending missionaries to the continent of Africa or the other parts of the heathen world'. The times were hardly propitious for such a new undertaking. Britain was entering upon the ninth year of her war against Revolutionary France, industrial discontent was rife, prices were high, and a novel income tax, which rose to 2s. in the pound on incomes of £200 a year and more, had just been introduced by the government. Nevertheless, the decision was taken at that meeting to establish what became known as the Church Missionary Society (see p. 116), and the tea-pot from which those first founders refreshed themselves on that occasion is still preserved by the Society.

In the words of John Venn, the Society was to operate 'on the Church principle, but not the High Church principle'. Since the Tractarian movement still lay in the future, this phrase was intended, not in a doctrinal sense, but in relation to the control of the Society. The Evangelicals were aware that they were a minority group within the Church, unable to exercise authority, and were determined, therefore, to retain their independence and not submit the Society to episcopal direction which traditional Church principles required. Nevertheless, the founders wanted the Society to work within the system of the Church. They would only employ episcopally ordained* clergymen, but as they indicated in the first *Account* of the Society, this raised a problem which had to be faced:

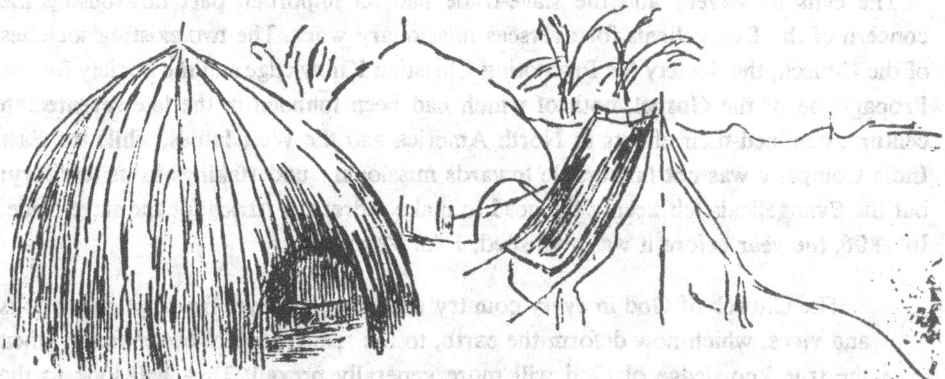

The rough sketch of his prison by James Hannington, an Evangelical who became the first Bishop of Eastern Equatorial Africa and was murdered in Uganda in 1885

> A difficulty has occurred in establishing missions according to the regular constitution of the Church of England, which it is necessary to state, in order to justify a part of the present institution which might else appear exceptionable. It is obvious that the Church of England can allow no persons to officiate in any respect as Ministers who have not been *episcopally ordained*. Episcopal ordination, bearing respect to the present improved state of society in this island, is justly conferred upon those only, whose education and learning qualify them for the rank the English clergy hold in society. It is evident, however, that a missionary, dwelling amongst savages rude and illiterate, does not require the same kind of talents, manners or learning, as are necessary in an officiating minister in England. But ordination admits not of distinctions correspondent to the degree of refinement in society. He who is once episcopally ordained, though with the sole view of acting as a missionary to the heathen, would possess the power of officiating, and holding any benefice to which he might be presented, in the English Church. This circumstance necessarily requires extreme caution in ordaining persons for the purposes of missions only. For what security can be afforded, that a person of inferior station, offering himself upon this ground for orders, is not influenced by the desire of a more elevated rank in society, or of a life of greater ease, rather than by a pure zeal for the salvation of the heathen?
>
> C. Hole, *Early History of the Church Missionary Society* (1896), App B.

The answer they adopted to the question, which was based upon a social rather than a religious difficulty, was to employ, when necessary, lay catechists in the mission field:

> To obviate this difficulty, which lies in the way of sending missionaries episcopally ordained, the conductors of the present institution have recourse to the expedient of sending their missionaries in the capacity of *catechists* only, where persons already in holy orders do not offer themselves, or circumstances do not justify an application for regular ordination.
>
> *Ibid.*

Other societies founded by Evangelicals to work within the Church were the Church Missions to Jews (1809), which came about through approaches made to them by Christian Jews; the Colonial and Continental Church Society (1838), which maintained chaplains in the colonies and in Europe; and the Church Pastoral Aid Society (1836), which had the aim of 'increasing the number of working clergymen in the Church of England, and encouraging the appointment of pious and discreet laymen as helpers to the clergy in duties not ministerial'. Nor was this all. Many Evangelicals were prepared to adopt a new attitude of co-operation with Nonconformists. Though the Church Missionary Society did not intend to do this, one of its original rules stated, 'A friendly intercourse shall be maintained with other Protestant societies engaged in the same benevolent design of propagating the Gospel of Jesus Christ'; and other societies came into being through Evangelical initiative in which churchmen and Nonconformists participated equally. The most important of these were the Religious Tract Society, founded in the same year as the Church Missionary Society, and the British and Foreign Bible Society five years later.

At first Clapham, which had provided the impetus that produced these societies, was their centre and treasury, but with the passing of the generation of Wilberforce and his friends, this was lost. The societies began to suffer from the lack of a central organization and place of meeting. Accordingly, a number of Evangelicals opened Exeter Hall in the Strand, which from 1831 until 1907 provided the societies with offices and halls for their meetings. Here also the seventh Earl of Shaftesbury and other later Evangelicals took part in assemblies devoted to securing the causes they had at heart. Exeter Hall, indeed, came to be used allusively as a description of their activities, and it exercised an important influence for the rest of the century:

> Midway between the Abbey of Westminster and the Church of the Knights Templar, twin columns, emulating those of Hercules, fling their long shadows across the strait through which the far-resounding Strand pours the full current of human existence into the deep recesses of Exeter Hall. Borne on that impetuous tide, the Mediterranean waters lift up their voices in a ceaseless swell of exultation or pathetic declamation. The changeful strain rises with the civilization of Africa, or becomes plaintive over the wrongs of chimney-boys, or peals anathemas against the successors of Peter, or in rich diapason calls the Protestant churches to awake and evangelize the world. Criticize, for there is no lack of extravagance. Laugh, for there is no stint of affectation. Yet refuse not to believe, that, grotesque as her appearance may occasionally be, Exeter Hall has a history, a doctrine and a prophecy of no common order.
>
> Sir James Stephen, *Essays in Ecclesiastical Biography* (1849), 582.

Success by the Evangelicals did not silence their opponents and critics. The zeal with which they sought to spread their message and win converts by the distribution of tracts, the organization of meetings and, above all, the preaching of sermons, won them much dislike and contempt. Later, the Tractarians were quick to accuse the

Evangelical clergy of neglecting pastoral work in favour of preaching. Thomas Mozley stigmatized the typical Evangelical preacher in these words:

> The great mass of people committed to his care he assumed to be utterly bad or hopelessly good . . . He delivered his message, and that was enough, for him at least. He could thus reserve his attention for a few. Relieved thus from the dull reiteration of house to house work, and from close parochial work generally, he became immobilized . . . The Evangelical preacher very soon discovered that his vocation was not in cottages or in hovels or in farm houses or in garrets and cellars . . . in dirty lanes and courts.
>
> T. Mozley, Reminiscences, *Chiefly of Oriel College and the Oxford Movement* (2 vols, 1882), I, 185.

This, however, was not true of many Evangelical clergymen and probably not true of most. In parishes all over the country the coming of an Evangelical incumbent meant a greater number of services and more frequent communicants, meetings for prayer and Bible-study, the distribution of coal and blankets to the poor, the visitation of the sick and the promotion of new standards of reverence and devotion. In 'Janet's Repentance', one of the stories in *Scenes of Clerical Life*, George Eliot spoke of the effect of the coming of the Revd Edgar Tryan as officiating curate at the Puddiford Chapel-of-Ease in the parish of Melby:

> Nevertheless, Evangelicalism had brought into palpable existence and operation in Melby society that idea of duty, that recognition of something to be lived for beyond the mere satisfaction of self, which is to the moral life what the addition of a great central ganglion is to animal life. No man can begin to mould himself on a faith or an idea without rising to a higher order of experience: a principle of subordination, of self-mastery, has been introduced into his nature; he is no longer a mere bundle of impressions, desires and impulses. Whatever might be the weaknesses of the ladies who pruned the luxuriance of their lace and ribbons, cut out garments for the poor, distributed tracts, quoted Scripture and defined the true Gospel, they had learned this—that there was a divine work to be done in life, a rule of goodness higher than the opinion of their neighbours; and if the notion of a heaven in reserve for themselves was a little too prominent, yet the theory of fitness for that heaven consisted in purity of heart, in Christ-like compassion, in the subduing of selfish desires. They might give the name of piety to much that was only puritanic egoism; they might call many things sin that were not sin; but they had at least the feeling that sin was to be avoided and

resisted, and colour-blindness, which may mistake drab for scarlet, is better than total blindness, which sees no distinction of colour at all.

George Eliot, *Scenes of Clerical Life* (World's Classics Edition, 1933), 319.

A common charge against the Evangelicals was that they were ignorant, unscholarly and limited in their approach to the Christian religion. It was a charge often made against them by the Tractarians and their later successors. Thus, H. P. Liddon wrote of them towards the end of the century:

> Partly in virtue of its very intensity, [the Evangelical movement] was, in respect of its advocacy of religious truth, an imperfect and one-sided movement. It laid stress only on such doctrines of Divine Revelation as appeared to its promoters to be calculated to produce a converting or sanctifying effect upon the souls of men. Its interpretation of the New Testament—little as its leaders ever suspected this—was guided by a traditional assumption as arbitrary and groundless as any tradition which it ever denounced. The real sources of its 'Gospel' were limited to a few chapters of St Paul's Epistles . . . understood in a manner which left much else in Holy Scripture out of account; and thus the Old Testament history, and even the life of our Lord Jesus Christ, as recorded by the Evangelists, were thrown comparatively into the background. The needs and salvation of the believer, rather than the whole revealed Will of Him in Whom we believe, was the governing consideration. As a consequence, those entire departments of the Christian revelation which deal with the corporate union of Christians with Christ in His Church and with the Sacraments, which by His appointment are the channels of His grace to the end of time, were not so much forgotten as unrecognized.

H. P. Liddon, *Life of E. B. Pusey* (4 vols, 1893–97), I, 255f.

It may seem that such criticism, expressed in this way, amounted to an accusation that the Evangelical interpretation and application of Christianity was not the same as that of its opponents. Every age has put forward its own conception of that religion, and the tenets which aroused firm and passionate support among Christians in Victorian times find decreasing acceptance nowadays. The Evangelicals had a coherent scheme of religion, and whatever men of learning might think, it appealed to many ordinary people. For them the Evangelicals had a message of love that won simple hearts. It taught them that if they would accept Christ as Saviour, then God with His love and compassion would forgive them and grant them the Kingdom of Heaven.

Nevertheless, the decline of the Evangelical movement was continually proclaimed. Mark Pattison forcibly insisted that this occurred before the inauguration of the Victorian period:

> In 1833 Evangelicalism was already effete. The helpless imbecility of Evangelical writing and preaching; their obvious want of power to solve, or even to apprehend, the questions of which they are nevertheless perpetually talking; their incapacity to explain the Scripture, while assuming the exclusive right to it; their conceit of being able to arrive at conclusions without premises; in a word, their intellectual weakness, contributed very greatly to the fall of the Evangelical school before a better-informed generation.
>
> Mark Pattison, *Essays* (2 vols, 1889), II, 1942.

Yet such assertions bear the mark of wishful thinking. The Evangelicals never became dominant in the Church, but they remained influential throughout the century. Indeed, in the middle years of the century, when J. B. Sumner, a convinced Evangelical, was Archbishop of Canterbury, Lord Palmerston was Prime Minister, and his adviser on ecclesiastical appointments was his stepson-in-law, the respected Lord Shaftesbury, they enjoyed a new phase of power. And for the rest of the century they were far from disappearing. The Church Missionary Society remained the largest Anglican missionary society, and the average parish, if not in Evangelical care, owed more to them than to any other movement.

3 The Reformers

While the Evangelical and other religious movements within the Church of England are comparatively well known, much less attention has been paid to the administrative reforms which took place during the nineteenth century. Yet these were far-reaching in their scope and vitally needed to enable the Church to meet the demands and face the difficulties of the new age. And their effect was at least as important as that of the better-known movements. Indeed, it has been suggested that, so far as any human power did save the Church, it was saved not by these movements, but by the administrative reforms.

Prominent among the names associated with these reforms was that of Lord Liverpool, the founder of Liberal Toryism and Prime Minister from 1812 to 1827. He was the first Prime Minister to remedy one of the worst surviving medieval abuses—the exploitation of high ecclesiastical preferment to requite the services of servants of the State. In the Middle Ages the State had made heavy demands on the resources of the Church: bishops had served as ministers and ambassadors and inferior clerics as clerks. The rise of an educated class of laymen in the sixteenth century had brought that to an end, but throughout the eighteenth century successive administrations had appointed bishops who would support government measures with their influence and vote in the House of Lords. Liverpool broke away from this tradition and made the suitability of men for the office his only consideration in filling bishoprics.

Lord Henley, in his epoch-making pamphlet, *A Plan of Church Reform*, commented that it was amazing that it should have been necessary for Liverpool to have to assert this principle:

> In truth, ... all parties have joined in considering Church Patronage as so much oil for greasing the works of government ... Nothing sets this in a more striking light than the credit which Lord Liverpool for a few disinterested appointments, in which, disregarding the powerful, he elevated unpretending merit and excellence to high places in the Church. This conduct was, no doubt, highly laudable in the individual Minister; but the mere fact of its having

attracted any attention is sufficient evidence of the corruption of the system.

Lord Henley, *A Plan of Church Reform* (1832), 55–8.

Doubtless it was easier for Liverpool and successive Prime Ministers, who followed the precedent he had set, to act in this way than it would have been for their predecessors, because the progressive secularization of life in the nineteenth century was making increasingly possible the differentiation of the Church as a spiritual society. There were now other and more attractive ways of gaining support for governments than by the use of ecclesiastical patronage. Yet if this action was more than ever possible, it was also more than ever urgent. The bishops should have been the leaders of the Church in the face of its many problems, yet as the Tractarian movement was particularly to show, many of them were incapable of acting in this way. E. B. Pusey, who recognized Liverpool as the first Prime Minister to nominate bishops out of principle, spoke of the situation produced by the appointments of the eighteenth century:

> In the last century persons were taken out of the priesthood for the higher office of Bishop; whence there grew up that habitual mistrust of Bishops which is not easily shaken off. The laity bartered their 'birthright for a mess of potage'. Church patronage was at the best employed for purposes of this world. The laity had the Bishops whom they desired, and when they had them despised them.

E. B. Pusey, *Councils of the Church* (1857), 14.

One of the first of the new sort of bishops nominated by Liverpool was Henry Ryder, whom he appointed to Gloucester in 1815 and translated to Lichfield in 1824. Ryder was also the first Evangelical to receive a bishopric, and he startled everyone, when he came to Lichfield, by plunging into Evangelistical work and preaching all over his diocese, especially in the expanding industrial areas. For twelve years he laboured in this diocese, then much larger than now, until he broke down and died from the strain of his work. Particularly he strove to forward the building of new churches to meet the needs of the growing population, and by the time of his death thirty had been built in Staffordshire alone. His words in 1832 expressed his constant concern for the poor in the towns under his charge:

> How often must the Urbicus of our days have to exclaim in the bitterness of his heart—Where alas are these my 'stray sheep'—stray from compulsion in the wilderness of this evil world; those poor whom I might instruct, according to the promise of making them wise unto eternal life?

W. Beresford, *Diocesan History of Lichfield* (1878), 277.

A more important bishop appointed by Liverpool was Charles James Blomfield, the man who has been called the hero of the reform movement in the Church. The son of an East Anglian schoolmaster, he had a distinguished academic and parochial career before Liverpool offered him in 1824, at the age of thirty-eight, the bishopric of Chester. Although its income, only £1,400 a year, was hardly sufficient for its responsibilities, Lady Spencer, the wife of his friend and patron, wrote to him:

> Don't be so indiscreet as to refuse it because it is a sadly poor one—remember it is the step which you must tread on to a richer one . . . I am impatient to see you seated on that bench, where you will be so admirably placed, and so usefully disposed of. If the Metropolitan is translated, which his looks portend, the Bishop of London replaces him; and who so likely as yourself, with all your London knowledge and experience, to be the Bishop of this diocese, if you *are* on the bench—but then you must be, or my plan can't take place. Seriously, Lord Spencer and I are on tiptoe to hear of your acceptance; for, though it may be present ruin, yet will it be *soon* future affluence. And why should you not keep your St Botolph?
>
> S. C. Carpenter, *op cit*, 90.

He found the diocese of Chester in a poor condition, but he did a great work of rehabilitation during his four years there. He set out to raise the standard of clerical life, to improve the preparation of the ordinands and to eradicate abuses, especially those of non-residence, though he himself had been allowed to retain his former London parish of St Botolph, Aldgate. In 1828 he became Bishop of London and held the post for nearly thirty years. His character and the impression he made on the sentiment of the time is illustrated in an early biographical note:

> His stature, when in the prime of life, was above the middle height, and his personal appearance was strongly expressive of the scholar and the man of business. The aspect of his brow and head impressed a sense of his perceptivity and mental power on even the most cursory beholder, and was considered by phrenologists as affording a splendid verification of their science. His manner seemed to strangers to be abrupt, and his demeanour haughty; but those who knew him best believed that his heart was kind, and his disposition cheerful, though occasionally beclouded in private by physical causes. He entertained the social circle with the fund of his anecdotes, the stores of his reading, and the versatility of his wit. He was a very early riser; and, by skilful management, found time for an amazing multitude of most efficient labours, and even for

literary pursuits. As a debater in Parliament whenever his official position required him to share in its discussions, he was vigorous and lucid. As a preacher, he combined the clearest statements of doctrinal truth, with the most forcible and persuasive inferences from them of practical obligation. He retained, indeed, the large revenues of his see, whose net annual value was recently returned by himself at £16,513, even after other prelates had consented to a limitation of theirs, but he distributed out of his abundance with an unsparing hand to church-building, the funds of schools, and the relief of the poorer clergy; and chiefly by life insurance provided for his six sons and five daughters. His 'infirmities' of which, in his first charge to the clergy of London, he professed himself, with a falling tear, to be 'deeply conscious,' were perhaps mainly attributable to his constitution of body, and the peculiar and increasing difficulties of the course he had to steer, from the time he became Bishop of London until his resignation. As might reasonably be expected, he left the world divided into two opposite parties in their opinions of his principles and conduct; and, as *The Times* (August 7th, 1857) remarked, when noticing his death, 'The day may yet be far distant when the boundary line will be finally adjusted between the opposite classes of those who indiscriminately admire him on the one hand, and criticize him unkindly on the other.'

J. W. C. Wand, *The Second Reform* (1953), 8.

When he came to London, Blomfield set out to get new churches built in such poor districts as Bethnal Green, Islington and St Pancras. In 1836 he founded a church-building society for the metropolis and made an appeal for the erection of fifty new churches. The idea was widely ridiculed, but the appeal met with an amazing success. Donations came in, and he himself built and endowed St Stephen's, Shepherds Bush, entirely at his own expense. And in 1843 Sir Robert Peel secured the passing of an Act of Parliament which facilitated the creation of new parishes for these churches. In all, some two hundred new churches were built and consecrated in London, chiefly through Blomfield's zeal and energy. It was a valiant effort to enable the Church to meet the needs of the growing population of the metropolis, and the money he raised was generally well spent; he had a reasonable concern for the dignity and architecture of the buildings he authorized. Nevertheless, four years after his death, a searching criticism of his policy was made in the *Christian Remembrancer*:

The late Bishop Blomfield, with characteristic energy and honesty, took up the problem [of Church extension], and tried to solve it, as he did every difficulty, by what he thought to be common sense. But in this, as in many other matters, commonplace sense is not common sense. The commonplace view of this Church extension is to consider it as an arithmetical sum. If 500 people in the country, or 2,000 people in a town, are enough for one parson to look after, there are given so many people, how many parsons do we want? If a town church holds 1,000 people, how many thousands are there in London without Church accommodation, and how many churches shall we want? This was Bishop Blomfield's method. This was what he approximately aimed at. But the very enunciation of such a problem condemned it. It was absolutely impossible to get either the men, the churches, or the money; and this the late Bishop of London lived to find out. But if he could not do everything, he could do something; if he could not build a brazen wall, he could stop a gap in the hedge here and there. So the Bethnal Green churches were built, and cheap churches were built about the suburbs; and something was done to overtake the daily increasing hordes of irreligion and vice. And at first some success was achieved. The first incumbents of these new churches were often men of energy, and sometimes of means; but that energy being but of flesh and blood, was not immortal; those means were not those of a Fortunatus; and somehow, Bishop Blomfield could not face a failure. He complained of his tools when his principle was wrong. He did not always encourage men in difficult positions, though few sympathized so warmly with those who were, or who said they were, successful. And so the great scheme of Church extension in London languished, and before the death of the late Bishop, it may be said to have passed out of official hands into those of private energy. Here and there a splendid church has been erected by private munificence, but the Metropolis Churches' Fund died of absolute inanition before its exemplary and excellent founder. Bishop Blomfield lived to see the rise and extinction of parochial subdivision on the old scale, and according to the old idea . . . When the district churches are built, it is impossible in towns to force the parochial system. People will go to church where they choose, not where they ought to go according to the Church theory. But it was with the clergy of the new districts that the break-down was most complete. Some disdained the arts by which popularity was to be won: and some were incapable of attracting their parishioners either by life, example or power; and when the late Bishop of London, by deserting those of his clergy who stuck by him on his charge of 1842, showed that it was the best policy to defy him as the Islington clergy did on that memorable occasion, he found some difficulty in manning his new churches, or at least in getting successors to his first incumbents. And we mention London only, because it fairly represents the system of minute subdivision of parishes. The plan as long as it lasts is this: Get a young and enthusiastic clergyman; set him down single-handed to build schools, compel him to do the whole work of the church, and keep up all its institutions, its lectures and library and night schools: let him have a wife and family, which gives a respectable air to the institution, and a Peel district and 150*l.* per annum. And this may be done once. A curate is always found to take a new church. He generally has small means, great spirits, and good principles. In a few years he is used up: the orange is sucked, and goes the way of all sucked oranges. And if this were all, the consequences would be rather favourable than otherwise to the Church. As the blood of martyrs is a fertilizing shower to the Church, so a succession of used-up incumbents is not without its moral effects. After all, to be ruined in health and pocket in a Peel district is in itself a kind of confessorship; and as to mere suffering, the axe and the stake are not perhaps so hard to endure as the daily cross of accumulating debts and difficulties which at last submerge the poor Peel incumbent. But the evil does not stop here . . .

Christian Remembrancer, December 1861, vol xlii, 472ff.

Another reform which Blomfield much wanted was the revival of the ancient Convocations* as assemblies which would be able to give direction to such general reform of the Church as he and several other bishops had undertaken in their dioceses. Eventually the Convocation of Canterbury began to discuss business again in 1850, and the Convocation of York followed its example in 1861. The clergy now had a means of expressing their opinion and taking action in a way that could not be done by Parliament. This reform, however, was not achieved without opposition, particularly from those who feared that the revival would give Blomfield and his supporters an opportunity to dominate the Church. Even a Broad Churchman like F. D. Maurice expressed a mild cynicism about their efforts:

Even if the Convocation should find out that it existed only to impose taxes on the clergy—which I fancy is the true idea of it—I cannot think that in a day when Blomfield is virtually their ruler, this office should be performed with any safety to that which is abidingly meant for the good of future generations. Everything would be sacrificed to the tastes, fears, or apparent advantages of the moment.

Frederick Maurice, *Life of Frederick Denison Maurice* (2 vols, 1885), I, 309.

Meanwhile, an important step had been taken towards the establishment of a central body to manage the finances of the Church and so make possible a thorough administrative reform of the Church. This was the setting up of a Commission by Sir Robert Peel in 1835 to consider reforms in the allotment of the Church's revenues. In a letter written on 12th January 1835 to Lord Harrowby, Peel announced his intentions with regard to the Commission:

> The immediate course I propose to pursue for the purpose of laying the safe foundations at least of progressive reform in the Church is the appointment of a Commission to which I should confidentially refer, on the avoidance of any great preferment, the consideration of those arrangements in detail which might best promote the object I have in view, and which Commission might also consider prospectively the arrangements which it might be advisable to adopt, either with the consent of those who have at present existing interests, or, if their consent cannot be had, on the occurrence of a vacancy.
>
> I think of constituting the Commission thus:
>
> | | |
> |---|---|
> | The Archbishop of Canterbury | The Lord Chancellor |
> | The Archbishop of York | Sir Robert Peel |
> | The Bishop of London | Mr Goulburn |
> | The Bishop of Lincoln | Mr Charles Wynn |
> | The Bishop of Gloucester | Sir Herbert Jenner |
>
> and, with your permission, yourself.

Norman Gash (ed), *The Age of Peel* (1968), 60–1.

The joint episcopal and ministerial membership was designed to make its recommendations acceptable to both Parliament and Church. It was established by Peel in February 1835, and when the Whigs were returned to office, they renewed the Commission in June of that year, replacing the Conservative ministerial members by Whigs. In the following year an Act of Parliament was passed, establishing a permanent body of Ecclesiastical Commissioners, who were empowered to hold and purchase lands and to prepare schemes for the alteration and redistribution of ecclesiastical revenues.

The most important immediate action taken by the permanent Commission was to adjust the incomes of the bishops, removing the serious inequalities which had existed between dioceses and establishing Ripon and Manchester as the first of the much-needed new bishoprics of the century; and to reduce the size of cathedral chapters* in order to apply their revenue to the provision of churches and clerical stipends* in populous areas. This diversion of wealth from the cathedrals was much desired by Blomfield:

> I traverse the streets of this crowded city with deep and solemn thoughts of the spiritual condition of its inhabitants. I pass the magnificent church which crowns the metropolis and is consecrated to the noblest of objects, the glory of God, and I ask myself in what degree it answers the object. I see there a dean* and three residentiaries* with incomes amounting in the aggregate to between £10,000 and £12,000 a year. I see, too, connected with the Cathedral twenty-nine clergymen whose offices are all but sinecures,* with an annual income of about £12,000 at the present moment and likely to be very much larger after the lapse of a few years. I proceed a mile or two to the east and north-east and find myself in the midst of an immense population, in the most wretched state of destitution and neglect, artisans, mechanics, labourers, beggars, thieves, to the number of at least 300,000. I find there, upon an average, about one church and one clergyman for every 8,000 or 10,000 souls; in some districts a much smaller amount of spiritual provision; in one parish, for instance, only one church and one clergyman for 40,000 people . . . I am told, you may not touch St Paul's. It is an ancient corporation, which must be maintained in its integrity. Not a stall can be spared. The duties performed there are too important to admit of any diminution in the number of those who perform them. One sermon a Sunday is preached every Sunday by a residentiary, and another by a clergyman appointed by the Bishop and paid by the Corporation of London; while the non-residentiaries either preach an occasional sermon on saints' days or pay a minor canon for preaching it. And yet if the principle of perfect integrity, as to numbers and property, is to be maintained, as the opponents of this measure assert, not a farthing must be taken from these splendid endowments, for which so little duty is performed, to furnish spiritual food to some of the thousands of miserable destitute souls that are perishing of famine in the neighbourhood of this abundance.
>
> Alfred Blomfield, *A Memoir of Charles James Blomfield* (2 vols, 1863), I, 225–6.

The measures of administrative reform, undertaken by governments and bishops, depended for their success upon the efforts of the parochial clergy. The backbone of the pastoral system of the Church of England in the new areas of population was still the traditional parish and the work of the incumbents and curates. John Wesley had never held any parochial appointment in the Church. He said, 'The world is my parish', and he found it impossible to organize his movement within the parochial framework; but the Church, for better or for worse, was committed to this system, and so reforms would have been of no avail unless a determined effort was made by the clergy themselves to operate the system properly. Fortunately, as the nineteenth century progressed, a new generation of clergymen began to replace the somewhat haphazard, lackadaisical approach to parochial responsibilities of the past by a new efficiency and thoroughness which gradually transformed beyond recognition the conception of pastoral duties.

Among the clergy who were the pioneers of this movement was W. F. Hook, who had found the situation in his parish so depressing when he became Vicar of Leeds. Within ten years, if he had not made the Church more popular there, he had at least given it a mission in this challenging district and ensured that it had the means to carry this out. Edward Jackson, who became one of his curates at Leeds Parish Church in 1846, later described the daily routine that Hook and his staff followed:

> We lived together to save money, so that we could have more to spend on the poor. We rose at six and within a few minutes were assembled for a short service wherein we blessed God for our preservation through the night and dedicated ourselves afresh to His service throughout the day. At half-past seven, two of us were at church, beginning the early morning service, which was regularly attended by a number of earnest souls, both young and old, rich and poor, some of whom came from a considerable distance. Before breakfast we had our own family worship. At nine the day-schools had to be opened with prayer and afterwards religious instruction given to the older scholars. From school the transition was naturally to the districts, where the anxiously-expected visits were made until half-ten, at which hour those of us who had not already been to Morning Prayer had to hasten to church to take the ordinary forenoon service, preceded by marriages and followed by baptisms and churchings, while the others continued to visit in their districts. In the afternoon, at three, came baptisms again, with churchings and burials, and a full choral service; the latter to be repeated at half-past seven, but now only read for the convenience of working people, and others, who could not attend earlier. At the last service in church only one curate was usually present, the rest being otherwise fully occupied, some with classes of candidates for Confirmation, or of communicants, others at evening schools, but all in one way or another. It was usually ten o'clock before we had wearily reached home, to eat our simple supper, have our

> night's devotion, and go gladly to rest. Sunday, however sacred, was no Sabbath, being the day least of all the seven a day of rest.
>
> E. Jackson, *The New Curate* (1869), 2.

A later clergyman, who also worked in an industrial town, was William Clavell Ingram, Vicar of St Matthew's, Leicester, from 1874 to 1892. He had a large nineteenth-century church, built when Leicester was changing from a market to a factory town, and a working-class parish with a population of about 14,000. Among the parish organizations he directed were the five Sunday schools which had a total attendance of over 1,500 children. One of his former curates wrote an account of them:

> On Friday night, after Evensong, he held a meeting of the Sunday School Teachers in the North Chapel of the Church, carefully explaining the lessons for the Sunday as arranged in the Lesson Book. This book was an adaptation of one drawn up by his predecessor, and was arranged by Mr Ingram to bring out the cycle of the Church's teaching. He gave much time and thought to its yearly re-editing. It was printed in Leicester and used in a great many parishes, and many clergy have expressed themselves largely indebted to him for the help received from it. Yearly examinations were held on it, and the competition between the scholars for a high place on the lists was most keen. On Sunday afternoon the elder members of the Sunday School assembled in church, and Mr Ingram catechised them very fully on the lesson of the day, but the most thrilling service was that held upon the last Sunday in the month, when all the children were present, and the Church was full to the doors—and the Vicar, rising fully to the occasion, brought out in a roar of children's voices the text, hymn and chief points they had received during the month, never omitting the portion of the Church catechism appointed in the Lesson Book. I shall never forget the exclamation of a dignitary of the Church that it was worth a long journey to be present at such a service.
>
> Anon., *A Memoir of William Clavell Ingram* (1903), 14–15.

An important factor in the higher standards set by the clergy in parochial work was the effect of the creation of the theological colleges. For long the clergy had mostly, though not entirely, come from men who had graduated at the universities, but many of them studied little theology there, and it was academic and not practical. There was a need to train the future clergy in habits of devotion and other demands of the work that lay ahead of them. Most of the theological colleges were founded to provide graduates with a course of professional training in preparation for ordination. The natural centres for such work were the cathedrals, fortunately finding a renewed purpose for themselves, corresponding to the revival of the parish churches. Chichester, which was established in 1839, was the first of these colleges, and over half a dozen others followed it during the century. There were other colleges, however, founded for men who had not been to a university, the first of these being St Bees, established in 1816. Such colleges broadened the character of the Church's ministry. Previously most of the clergy had come from a fairly narrow class of society, but this became decreasingly so during the Victorian age. It was a development which did not meet with general approval:

> We want a cheap and rough-and-ready clergy. This is the last invention of the day,—the very newest form of 'evangelizing the masses' . . . But the evil does not stop here; not only is the clerical *status*, but the clerical *morale* lowered. Premiums are held out to uneducated *alumni* of the cheap colleges to enter into holy orders, and all the evils of the Mendicant orders are introduced into the purer and reformed branch of the Church. It is a rise in the social scale for a linen-draper's clerk to become a reverend gentleman, and there will never be wanting candidates for the ministry if you lower the standard. But these recruits bring into the army of the Church not only the manners but the moral tone of the class which they represent. A socialist English clergy is no remote possibility. In the middle ages the Mendicants always headed the social *jacqueries*, and the brethren of the free spirit were popular favourites because they represented and encouraged the popular discontent with endowments, settled income, and landed inheritance. We deprecate the coming of that day, or the triumph of those principles, which shall encourage the rise of such an element in the clerical hierarchy of England. When clergymen clamour for the equalization of the poor rate, or take up the cause of the costermongers against the law, they forget that they are playing the game of socialism.
>
> *Christian Remembrancer*, December 1861, vol xlii, 474, 475.

It was vital for the Church also to find new aims and methods at the top. The great 'remodeller of the episcopate' (as John William Burgon, Dean of Chichester 1876–88, described him) was Samuel Wilberforce, son of the philanthropist and Bishop of Oxford from 1845 to 1869. He set a fresh guide for the pastoral work of the bishops. Among the pioneering achievements he initiated in his diocese were the insistence upon a new standard of vocation and fitness for those whom he ordained, the administration of the rite of confirmation with greater earnestness, the holding of missions to groups of parishes and the organization of diocesan societies for church building, spiritual guidance and the augmentation of poor benefices. He never spared himself and made searching rules for his own conscience in the conduct of his duties:

> The first great *necessity* seems to me to be to maintain a devotional temper. The first great *peril*—SECULARITY. To guard against this by self-examination and, above all, by living in prayer. Trusting in God's help, I resolve, as my universal rule, when not hindered by illness or some impossibility, to secure at least one hour before breakfast for devotional exercises. Next, as my great fear is acting with an eye to men and myself, rather than to God, I resolve:—Often to set my conduct, principles, etc in the light of the coming day; and try thus to form myself in the habit of acting under God's eye. Mem. to examine myself (1) next morning rather than at night when weary: (2) on my resolutions generally. To form a regular systematic habit of intercession for my clergy, etc.
>
> A. R. Ashwell & Reginald G. Wilberforce, *Life of Samuel Wilberforce* (3 vols, 1880–2), I, 319f.

4 The Tractarians

The Tractarian movement began, according to John Henry Newman (1801–90), Vicar of St Mary's Church, Oxford, with an assize sermon preached in that church on 'National Apostasy' in July 1833 by John Keble (1792–1866), who was soon to be Professor of Poetry in the University. Keble had been aroused by the government's plan to suppress ten bishoprics of the Church of Ireland, which was a Protestant establishment in a largely Roman Catholic country:

> One of the most alarming [omens of an Apostate mind in a nation] is the growing indifference, in which men indulge themselves to other men's religious sentiments. Under the guise of charity and toleration we are come almost to this pass; that no difference, in matters of faith, is to disqualify for our approbation and confidence, whether in public or domestic life. Can we conceal it from ourselves, that every year the practice is becoming more and more common, of trusting men unreservedly in the most delicate and important matters, without one serious inquiry, whether they do not hold principles which make it impossible for them to be loyal to their Creator, Redeemer and Sanctifier? Are not offices conferred, partnerships formed, intimacies entered upon—nay, (what is almost too painful to think of) do not parents commit their children to be educated, do they not encourage them to intermarry, in houses on which Apostolic Authority would rather teach them to set a mark, as unfit to be entered upon by a faithful servant of Christ?
>
> 'National Apostasy', No. 6 of *Sermons Academical and Occasional* (2nd ed, Oxford, 1848). Preached at St Mary's Church, Oxford, before his Majesty's Judges of Assize, 14th July 1833, in H. Bettenson, *Documents of the Christian Church* (1943), 433–4.

Keble's alarm was shared by other churchmen. The repeal of the Test and Corporation Acts in 1828 and the emancipation of Roman Catholics the next year seemed a challenge to the Church. The passing of the Reform Bill in 1832 gave the vote to a greater number of Nonconformists, many of whom were very hostile to the Church. There were prevalent demands that the Church should be deprived of its powers and privileges and its endowments diverted to other uses, which aroused among churchmen suspicions of the Ecclesiastical Commission and other financial reforms. There seemed to be a real fear that the Church was in danger.

This apprehension was keenly felt in Oxford, and within a few weeks after Keble's sermon, Newman and a number of his friends, among whom was Edward Bouverie Pusey (1800–82), Professor of Hebrew in the University, began to issue the long series of *Tracts for the Times*. Tract I, *Thoughts on the Ministerial Commission Respectfully Addressed to the Clergy*, was written by Newman. This extract contains his main argument:

> Now then let me come at once to the subject which leads me to address you. Should the Government and Country so far forget their GOD as to cast off the Church, to deprive it of its temporal honours and substance, *on what* will you rest the claim of respect and attention which you make upon your flocks? Hitherto you have been upheld by your birth, your education, your wealth, your connexions; should these secular advantages cease, on what must CHRIST'S Ministers depend? Is not this a serious practical question? We know how miserable is the state of religious bodies not supported by the State. Look at the Dissenters on all sides of you, and you will see at once that their Ministers, depending simply upon the people, become the *creatures* of the people. Are you content that this should be your case? Alas! can a greater evil befall Christians, than for their teachers to be guided by them, instead of guiding? How can we 'hold fast the form of sound words' and 'keep that which is committed to our trust', if our influence is to depend simply on our popularity? Is it not our very office to *oppose* the world? Can we then allow ourselves to *court* it? to preach smooth things and prophesy deceits? to make the way of life easy to the rich and indolent, and to bribe the humbler classes by excitements and strong intoxicating doctrine? Surely it must not be so;—and the question recurs, on *what* are we to rest our authority, when the State deserts us?
>
> CHRIST has not left His Church without claim of its own upon the attention of men. Surely not. Hard Master He cannot be, to bid us oppose the world, yet give us no credentials for so doing. There are some who rest their divine mission on their own unsupported assertion; others, who rest it upon their popularity; others, on their success; and others, who rest it upon their temporal distinctions. This last case has, perhaps, been too much our own; I fear we have neglected the real ground on which our authority is built,—OUR APOSTOLIC DESCENT.
>
> We have been born, not of blood, nor of the will of the flesh, nor of the will of

man, but of GOD. The LORD JESUS CHRIST gave His SPIRIT to His Apostles; they in turn laid their hand on those who should succeed him; and these again on others; and so the sacred gift has been handed down to our present Bishops, who have appointed us as their assistants, and in some sense representatives.

J. H. Newman, *Thoughts on the Ministerial Commission Respectfully Addressed to the Clergy* (1833), in W. G. Hutchison, *The Oxford Movement* (1907), 7–8.

This defence of the apostolic succession* was followed by other tracts in rapid succession, upholding the Church of England as a divine institution and expounding the Book of Common Prayer as a rule of faith. They obtained a wide circulation, and their effect was enormous. Though the movement soon gained many other supporters, Newman remained its dominant figure. By nature sceptical, he had come under Evangelical influences in his youth, and consequently he held that men knew God by intuition, if at all. He had no great learning and was never really constructive, but he had charm. He magnetized and attracted the young. St Mary's was the University Church, and during the 1830s his influence there was immense. Long afterwards Matthew Arnold recalled the impression Newman had made then:

> Forty years ago he was in the very prime of life; he was close at hand to us at Oxford; he was preaching in St Mary's pulpit every Sunday; he seemed about to transform and to renew what was for us the most national and natural institution in the world, the Church of England. Who could resist the charm of that spiritual apparition, gliding in the dim afternoon light through the aisles of St Mary's, rising into the pulpit, and then, in the most entrancing of voices, breaking the silence with words and thoughts which were a religious music,—subtle, sweet, mournful? I seem to hear him still, saying: 'After the fever of life, after wearinesses and sicknesses, fightings and despondings, languor and fretfulness, struggling and succeeding; after all the changes and chances of this troubled, unhealthy state,—at length comes death, at length the white throne of God, at length the beatific vision.'

Matthew Arnold, *Discourses in America* (1885), 139–140.

The religious position which Newman proclaimed in tracts and sermons was that of the *Via Media*, the belief that the Church of England by the providence of God held an intermediate position between Protestantism and Romanism. Directing criticisms equally 'against Popery and Dissent', he appealed to the ancient fathers of undivided Christendom. Such conservatism would not have gained him the ear of the young men; they listened to him because he was also revolutionary. For him the Church of

The University Church of St Mary the Virgin, Oxford

England had wonderfully survived the Reformation with its Catholic creed and ministry unimpaired, but these had become obscured through the growth of Protestant practice. The Church must shake this off and become faithful to its true nature. He wanted to forget the eighteenth century ('that dreadful century', he called it) and move on from a more distant past:

> I never expect the system of Laud to return but I do expect the due continuation and development of his principles . . . the so-called union of the Church and State as it then existed had been a wonderful and most gracious phenomenon in Christian history . . . a realization of the Gospel in its highest perfection when both Caesar and St Peter know and fulfil their office . . . Charles is the King, Laud the Prelate, Oxford the sacred city of this principle.
>
> J. H. Newman, 'How to Accomplish It', *Discussions and Arguments on Various Subjects* (1873), 22.

The Tractarians, however, soon began to have their opponents. Their attempts to prevent the liberal clergyman, R. D. Hampden, becoming Regius Professor of Divinity in 1836 aroused antagonism, and so did the publication the next year of the *Remains* of Newman's intimate friend, Richard Hurrell Froude (1803–36), in which he attacked the Protestant reformers and praised clerical celibacy and devotion to the Virgin Mary. Indeed, among the Tractarians there was gradually arising a party which tended more and more to submission to the Roman Catholic Church, prominent among these newcomers being W. G. Ward (1812–82), a fellow of Balliol College. In 1839 Newman himself began to have doubts about the claims of the Church of England. These took a typically academic form. He had very little personal knowledge of the contemporary Roman Catholic Church, but during the long vacation that year he studied the history of fifth-century heresies and seemed to find there 'Christendom of the sixteenth and nineteenth centuries reflected' in an alarming way:

> It was difficult to make out how the Eutychians* or Monophysites* were heretics, unless Protestants and Anglicans were heretics also; difficult to find arguments against the Tridentine* Fathers, which did not tell against the Fathers of Chalcedon*; difficult to condemn the Popes of the sixteenth century, without condemning the Popes of the fifth. The drama of religion, and the combat of truth and error, were ever one and the same. The principles and proceedings of the Church now, were those of the Church then; the principles and proceedings of heretics then, were those of Protestants now. I found it so,—almost fearfully; there was an awful similitude, more awful, because so silent and unimpassioned, between the dead records of the past and the feverish chronicle of the present. The shadow of the fifth century was on the sixteenth. It was like a spirit rising from the troubled waters of the old world, with the shape and lineaments of the new.
>
> J. H. Newman, *Apologia Pro Vita Sua* (1908), 115.

Though soon afterwards Newman's attention was drawn to an even more striking comparison with other heretics, the Donatists,* he stifled his doubts; but in 1841 the loyalty of the Tractarians was tried by the scheme for a bishopric in Jerusalem approved by Parliament. The bishopric was set up by the joint efforts of England and Prussia to serve the Anglicans and Protestants in the Middle East and North Africa. The scheme provided that the bishop was to be nominated by England and Prussia alternately. The Tractarians immediately objected to such a virtual union with a Protestant body without guarantees for the preservation of Church order or doctrine. It gravely weakened Newman's faith in the Catholic mission of the Church of England:

> At the very time that the Anglican Bishops were directing their censure upon me for avowing an approach to the Catholic Church ... they were on the other

> hand fraternising, by their act or by their sufferance, with Protestant bodies, and allowing them to put themselves under an Anglican Bishop without any renunciation of their errors or regard to the due reception of baptism and confirmation: while there was great reason to suppose that the said Bishop was intended to make converts from the orthodox Greeks, and the schismatical Oriental bodies.
>
> *Ibid*, 142–3.

It was partly to induce his followers and especially the younger men to remain loyal to the Church of England that Newman wrote in 1841 his famous Tract 90, *Remarks on Certain Passages in the Thirty-Nine Articles*, in which he tried to show that they were 'patent of a Catholic interpretation'. This is his comment on the Thirty-First Article:

> Article XXXI.—'The sacrifice of Masses, in the which it was commonly said, that the priest did offer Christ for the quick and the dead, to have remission of pain or guilt, were blasphemous fables and dangerous deceits'.
>
> Nothing can show more clearly than this passage that the Articles are not written against the creed of the Roman Church, but against actual existing errors in it, whether taken into its system or not. Here the sacrifice of the *Mass* is not spoken of; in which the special question of doctrine would be introduced; but '*the sacrifice of Masses*', certain observances, for the most part private and solitary, which the writers of the Articles knew to have been in force in time past, and saw before their eyes, and which involved certain opinions and a certain teaching. Accordingly the passage proceeds, 'in which it *was commonly said*', which surely is a strictly historical mode of speaking . . .
>
> These sacrifices are said to be 'blasphemous fables and pernicious impostures'. Now the 'blasphemous fable' is the teaching that there is a sacrifice for sin other than Christ's death, and that masses are that sacrifice. And the 'pernicious imposture' is the turning this belief into a means of filthy lucre . . . On the whole, then, it is conceived that the Article before us neither speaks against the Mass in itself, nor against its being an offering, though commemorative, for the quick and the dead for the remission of sin (especially since the decree of Trent says that 'the fruits of the Bloody Oblation are through this most abundantly obtained: so far is the latter from detracting in any way from the former'); but against it being viewed, on the one hand, as independent of or distinct from the Sacrifice on the Cross, which is blasphemy; and, on the other, its being directed to the

emolument of those to whom it pertains to celebrate it, which is imposture in addition.

W. G. Hutchison, *op cit*, 252–8.

Public opinion was really alarmed by the 'Jesuitry' of the suggested interpretations of the Articles. The heads of the colleges at Oxford made a protest, and questions were asked in Parliament. The Bishop of Oxford intervened, and Newman agreed to bring the *Tracts* to an end. The episode brought general condemnation upon the Tractarians, and for Newman it was an overwhelming blow. Many years later he wrote:

> I saw indeed clearly that my place in the Movement was lost; public confidence was at an end; my occupation was gone. It was simply an impossibility that I could say anything henceforth to good effect, when I had been posted up by the marshal on the buttery hatch of every College of my University, after the manner of discommoned pastry-cooks, and when in every part of the country and every class of society, through every organ and occasion of opinion, in newspapers, in periodicals, at meetings, in pulpits, at dinner-tables, in coffee-rooms, in railway carriages, I was denounced as a traitor who had laid his train and was detected in the very act of firing it against the time-honoured Establishment ... Confidence in me was lost;—but I had already lost full confidence in myself. Thoughts had passed over me a year and a half before, which for the time had profoundly troubled me. They had gone: I had not less confidence in the power and the prospects of the Apostolical movement than before; not less confidence than before in the grievousness of what I called the 'dominant errors' of Rome: but how was I any more to have absolute confidence in myself? how was I to have confidence in my present confidence? how was I to be sure that I should always think as I thought now? I felt that by this event a kind Providence had saved me from an impossible position in the future.

J. H. Newman, *Apologia*, 173–4.

Now that his usefulness in the Church of England had been ended, he gradually gave up his position in Oxford from 1841 onwards, living from 1842 at the neighbouring village of Littlemore, which was at that time part of the ecclesiastical parish of St Mary, Oxford. He had built a house and a small church at Littlemore, and he now set up a semi-monastic establishment there and lived in retirement with a few friends. He resigned the incumbency of St Mary's in 1843. Those whom he gathered around him at Littlemore were mostly the younger men whose Romeward thoughts were causing him and their friends considerable anxiety. Later he said of those years with them there:

I interposed from fidelity to my clerical engagements, and from duty to my Bishop, and from the interest which I was bound to take in them, and from belief that they were premature or excited ... I kept some of them back for several years from being received into the Catholic Church. Even when I had given up my living, I was still bound by my duty to their parents or friends, and I did not forget still to do what I could for them.

Ibid, 177.

Meanwhile, the Tractarian movement had received further blows. In May 1843 Pusey was suspended from preaching within the University for two years on account of a sermon, entitled 'The Holy Eucharist a Comfort to the Penitent', which he preached in Christ Church Cathedral before the University. He himself described its object and aim sixteen years later:

It implied rather than stated even the doctrine of the Real Objective Presence,* and was written chiefly by the language of the Fathers. Its one object was to inculcate the love of our Redeemer for us sinners in the Holy Eucharist, both as a Sacrament and as a commemorative Sacrifice. As a Sacrament, in that He, our Redeemer, God and Man, vouchsafes to be 'our spiritual food and sustenance in that holy Sacrament'. As a commemorative Sacrifice,* in that He enables us therein to plead to the Father that one meritorious Sacrifice on the Cross, which He, our High Priest, unceasingly pleads in His own Divine Person in Heaven.

E. B. Pusey, *University Sermons* (2 vols, 1859), I, vi.

The next year Ward published *The Ideal of a Christian Church* in which he strongly praised the Roman Catholic Church. The University deprived him of his degrees for heresy in 1845, and he became a Roman Catholic in the same year. A simultaneous attempt, however, to condemn *Tract 90* failed. Newman still had his supporters in the University, as A. P. Stanley wrote to his sister:

It is very remarkable to observe how peculiar a feeling is excited the moment that the slightest attempt is made to eject Newman, as if men had an instinctive fear of touching even a hair of his head. Men who had been prepared to sacrifice Ward without a struggle recoiled in horror when they found that they were called upon to sacrifice Newman too.

R. E. Prothero, *Life and Correspondence of Arthur Penrhyn Stanley* (2 vols, 1893), I, 336.

By now Newman was, as he said, 'on my death-bed as regards my membership with the Anglican Church'. His position had been untenable since the storm aroused by

Tract 90. He spent his last months in the Church in satisfying his mind through writing his *Essay on the Development of Christian Doctrine.* Later he was to state in justification of his change of attitude towards the Churches of England and Rome:

> I was not a concealed Romanist during the whole, or any part of the years in question. For the first four years (up to Michaelmas 1839) I honestly wished to benefit the Church of England at the expense of the Church of Rome. For the second four years I wished to benefit the Church of England without prejudice to the Church of Rome. At the beginning of the ninth year (Michaelmas 1843) I began to despair of the Church of England, and gave up all clerical duty; and then what I wrote and did was influenced by the mere wish not to injure it, and not by the wish to benefit it. At the beginning of the tenth year I distinctly contemplated leaving it, but I also distinctly told my friends that it was in my contemplation. Lastly, during the last half of that tenth year I was engaged in writing a book (*Essay on Development*) in favour of the Roman Church, and indirectly against the English; but even then, till it was finished, I had not absolutely intended to publish it, wishing to reserve to myself the chance of changing my mind when the argumentative views which were actuating me had been distinctly brought out before me in writing. I wish this statement, which I make from memory, and without consulting any document, severely tested by my writings and doings, as I am confident it will, on the whole, be borne out, whatever real or apparent exceptions (I suspect none) have to be allowed by me in detail.
>
> J. H. Newman, *op cit*, 186.

Now that he had written himself out of the Church of England, the way was clear for Newman to seek a solution for his perplexities by finding refuge in a Church which seemed to have none. He was received into the Roman Catholic Church in 1845 and almost immediately issued his *Essay* in defence of his change of allegiance. He was preceded or followed by several well-known Tractarian clergymen. The secession brought to an end the first phase of the Tractarian movement which had been so closely centred upon Oxford. Disaster struck the group when only a short time before its pioneers had looked as if they were close to triumph. In 1841, after the discontinuance of the *Tracts*, a leading article in *The Times* newspaper had said:

> Their teaching has now sunk deeply into the heart of the Church of England; it has acquired not merely a numerical, but a moral power and influence, which must henceforth make it impossible for any statesman to despise and overlook,

> and highly indiscreet unnecessarily to alienate, this element in the constitution of society. The younger clergy are said to be very generally of this school; it has no want of advocates among their seniors; it has penetrated into both Houses of Parliament; and we are confidently informed (we suppose, therefore, upon some foundation) that it has met with countenance from the Bishops themselves. It has completely succeeded in awakening in the Church that vital spirit of reaction, the necessity for which called it into existence. We hear nothing *now* of a demand for the admission of Dissenters into the Universities, of proposals to abolish subscription to the Thirty-Nine Articles, or of contemplated changes in the Liturgy; or, if we do still hear of them, the manner in which they are received, as contrasted with their popularity in 1833, illustrates the completeness of the victory still more forcibly.
>
> *The Times*, 6th March 1841.

Less than five years later, however, this had all changed. The destruction of the Tractarian movement at Oxford had deprived it of its chance of securing its aims in the University. Its eclipse made way for new ideas. There was a weariness with religious strife, and the obsolete condition of the University had been revealed. Henceforward liberal theology and liberal demands for academic reform grew steadily in power and influence. Once-devout Tractarians, who could not follow the path taken by Ward and Newman, turned with varying enthusiasm towards the liberals. One of these was Mark Pattison (1813–84), who said of Newman's departure from Oxford:

> It was a deliverance from the nightmare which had oppressed Oxford for fifteen years. For so long it had been given over to discussions unprofitable in themselves, and which had entirely diverted our thoughts from the true business of the place ... From that moment dates the regeneration of the University. Our thoughts reverted to their proper channel, that of the work we had to do ... We became aware how incompetent we were for it, and how narrow and incompetent was the character of the instruction with which we had been hitherto satisfied ... The great discoveries of the last half-century in chemistry, physiology, etc., were not even known by report to any of us. Science was placed under a ban by the theologians, who instinctively felt that it was fatal to their speculations ... The abject deference fostered by theological discussion for authority ... was incompatible with the free play of intellect which enlarges knowledge, creates science, and makes progress possible. In a word, the period of Tractarianism had been a

> period of obscurantism, which cut us off from the general movement; an eclipse which had shut out the light of the sun in heaven.

M. Pattison, *Memoirs* (1885), 236–8.

Another of these disenchanted Tractarians was James Anthony Froude (1818–94), the historian brother of Richard Hurrell Froude. During the time that Newman was at Littlemore, Froude had taken to studies of his own which had led him to suspect the Tractarians of obscurantism and anti-intellectualism partly brought about through a reaction against contemporary developments:

> This became clear to me, that the Catholic revival in Oxford, spontaneous as it seemed, was part of a general movement which was going on all over Europe. In France, in Holland, in Germany, intellect and learning had come to conclusions from which religion and conscience were recoiling. Pious Protestants had trusted themselves upon the Bible as their sole foundation. They found their philosophers and professors assuming that the Bible was a human composition—parts of it of doubtful authenticity, other parts bearing marks on them of the mistaken opinions of the age when these books were written; and they were flying terrified back into the Church from which they had escaped at the Reformation, like ostriches hiding their heads in a bush. Yet how could the Church, as they called it, save them? If what the philosophers were saying was untrue, it could be met by argument. If the danger was real, they were like men caught in a thunder-storm, flying for refuge to a tree which only the more certainly would attract the lightning.

J. A. Froude, 'Oxford Counter-Reformation', *Short Studies*, IV, 312.

As for the man who had done so much to make and break the movement, the elusive and puzzling Newman, an early post-Tractarian theologian, J. B. Mozley (1813–78), writing just after Newman's secession, accurately divined the weak part of his career in the Church of England. It was, he said, that Newman, despite his Evangelical conversion, had never become a sound member of the Church and, like John Wesley, had never understood its conception of the pastoral office:

> He did not energize as a parish priest, but as an author. His sermons were addressed to a University audience, to the world in general . . . Mr Newman had weekly communions and daily prayers; and he had the church at Littlemore with its daily duties . . . But all this was a thing attached to his great position, as a religious mover, and not that position to it. Mr Newman had one line—that of a spreader of opinions and former of public thought. And this line, however

appropriate a one, was still one which kept the Church distant as it were to his mind, and did not bring her near him.

J. B. Mozley, 'The Recent Schism', *Christian Remembrancer*, January 1846, vol xi, 179.

Yet, despite its weaknesses and failures, the Tractarianism of those days in Oxford had evolved a refined, spiritual conception of the Church of England which long continued to exercise an influence. This was expressed in a very attractive way by J. H. Shorthouse, the author of *John Inglesant* (1881), a novel set with sympathetic understanding in the religious life of the seventeenth century and yet owes much to the afterglow of Tractarianism. The last words he put into the mouth of his romantic hero are:

> The English Church, as established by the law of England, offers the supernatural to all who choose to come. It is like the Divine Being Himself, whose sun shines alike on the evil and on the good. Upon the altars of the Church the divine presence hovers as surely, to those who believe it, as it does upon the splendid altars of Rome. Thanks to circumstances the way is open; it is barred by no confession, no human priest. Shall we throw this aside? ... It is not even a question of religious freedom only; it is a question of learning and culture in every form. I am not blind to the peculiar dangers that beset the English Church. I fear that its position, standing, as it does, a mean between two extremes, will engender indifference and sloth; and that its freedom will prevent its preserving a discipline and organising power, without which any community will suffer grievous loss; nevertheless, as a Church it is unique; if suffered to drop out of existence, nothing like it can ever take its place.

5 The Ritualists

Though the Tractarians lost control of Oxford through Newman's defection, the movement was not, as many had thought it would be, destroyed by the event. The number of followers who accompanied him Romewards was much fewer than the authorities of that Church had hopefully expected. The movement remained strong because it retained some of its most prominent figures, the most important being Pusey. Newman had at first thought his example would be followed by Pusey, but there was never the slightest prospect of it. To Newman he wrote in 1846:

> You have but one wish for me; I cannot see otherwise than I have seen these many years; I have come to think otherwise in some details; but as to the one point on which it all turns, I am no nearer thinking that the English Church is no part of the true Church or that inter-communion with Rome is essential or that the present claims of Rome are Divine. I earnestly desire the restoration of unity, but I cannot throw myself into the practical Roman system, nor renounce what I believe our gracious Lord acknowledges. And so I must go on, with joy at the signs of deepening life among us, and distress at our losses, and amazement that Almighty God vouchsafes to employ me for anything, and thinking it less than I ought to expect when everything is brought to a contrary issue from what I desire.

H. P. Liddon, *Life of E. B. Pusey* (4 vols, 1893–7), II, 510.

The leadership of the movement now naturally devolved upon him, and its members were nicknamed the 'Puseyites'. He did much to prevent a serious split in the Church of England, both then and a few years later when the Gorham Case brought further conversions to the Roman Catholic Church. His great contribution towards calming the situation was his moderate attitude. While he remained firm in his disavowal of the papal claims, he would not join in open anti-Roman expressions of opinion. This brought him under the suspicion of really possessing Roman sympathies and led to accusations of evasiveness against him. William Palmer (1811–79), who was perhaps the outstanding Tractarian theologian at Oxford and was strongly opposed to both

Popery and Dissent, later wrote of the misapprehensions he felt concerning Pusey's position at this time:

> I should gladly have seen Pusey attempt to reform mistakes introduced by Newman, and endeavouring to correct, instead of seeming to go along with, the ultra-Tractarian mistakes . . . but in the end I became satisfied that the position he occupied was for the good of the Church . . . He had to control a very uncertain party, open to Newman's influence for some time—a party which was unsettled in principle and might easily be driven into secession . . . I should myself have often been in favour of a sterner and more direct policy towards all who shared in semi-Romanizing and Ritualistic opinions, and whom Pusey conciliated; but my own opinions were proved to be faulty by the result; for by mild methods the Church has been saved from further disruption and retains all the energies which a different mode of proceedings might have lost.
>
> William Palmer, *Supplement to a Narrative of Events Connected With Tracts for the Times* (1883), 240–41.

Moreover, during the decade in which the Tractarian movement had flourished at Oxford, it had, year by year, taken a firm hold upon the affections and practice of a large number of young men there. Robert Gregory (1819–1911), later Dean of St Paul's Cathedral, who came from a Nottingham Methodist family and was an undergraduate at Corpus Christi College, Oxford, from 1840 to 1843, later described the influence the movement had upon himself and others:

> The many undergraduates who were under the influence of the teaching of the *Tracts for the Times* were very strict in their attention to religious observances. During the whole of my undergraduate days my Sundays were spent as follows (and I have no reason to suppose that what I and some other members of my college did was at all different to what was done in other colleges): I went to the Celebration at St Mary's at seven o'clock, to College Chapel at eight, to the University service at ten and again at two, to Newman's service at St Mary's at four, and to College Chapel at seven; whilst on week-days I generally was present at College Chapel both at Matins and Evensong . . . The more enthusiastic of the young men, influenced by the *Tracts for the Times*, actively spread their opinions amongst their brother undergraduates, and some of them regularly attended the weekly tea-parties which Newman had in Oriel; but this I never did.
>
> Robert Gregory, *Autobiography* (1912), 25–6.

Many of these young men became, like Gregory, ordained and formed an increasingly important proportion of the clergy of the Church. They went out into parishes all over the country and endeavoured to put into practice the beliefs they had heard in Tractarian sermons and lectures at Oxford and the observances they had come to know at St Mary's and Littlemore. Thomas Mozley (1806–93), Newman's pupil and later his brother-in-law, came to know as an incumbent in rural Wiltshire the difficulties facing the clergy there when they tried to follow the teaching of the *Tracts* in the early days of the movement:

> We have only to imagine the not uncommon case of a young clergyman cast in a remote and secluded agricultural parish. He had to invite his parishioners to daily service, when every one of them was all day at work, generally far away from the church. He had to inculcate fasting, when most of them fasted already in the poverty and scantiness of their daily fare. He had to invite to confession those whose daily practice and antecedents were already well before the eyes of their neighbours. He had to invite to formal unity persons born and bred in schism, when they could not but prefer a good understanding between all opinions and sects, which it was not easy, if desirable, to interrupt. He had to urge the new doctrine in season and out of season, especially to the few educated neighbours who could understand him, and who settled the question by reducing their intercourse to occasional and unavoidable civilities. As often as not he found his own household incapable of going along with him. His wife had children to look after, and his servants did no more than the work absolutely required.
>
> Perhaps in spite of every obstacle he persisted. He had the church day after day, year after year, to himself alone, and perhaps two or three school children. His people were then told by authorities he was accustomed to respect that he was making an idol of the church, and that he prayed like the Pharisees in the synagogue instead of in his own chamber. He fasted after some fashion, and found himself incapable of work; not only weak but light-headed. He found his elder clerical neighbours generally dead against him, and the squires only too glad of the excuse to have nothing to do with him. If he tried weekly communion, it was with results too sad to tell.
>
> T. Mozley, *Reminiscences Chiefly of Oriel College and the Oxford Movement* (2 vols, 1882), I, 409–10.

Nevertheless, such standard-bearers of the Tractarian cause were not to be deterred from their efforts. They continued to persevere, with the result that, at the very time when the movement was crippled at Oxford and had lost its original form forever, it was beginning to assume a more general character and to exercise an increasing influence in the Church as a whole. This development inevitably brought about a change in the emphasis of the movement. It left the *Tracts* behind and became commonly known as the Oxford Movement or the Anglo-Catholic Movement. The *Tracts* had been largely theological in content and were addressed to the shepherds rather than to the sheep. The movement now became more pastoral in its concern, applying itself to the needs of parochial worship and work rather than to the debates in the University. The questions of authority and tradition in the doctrinal relationships of the Churches of England and Rome, which had caused Newman such meticulous concern, no longer took a prominent part in the new phase of the movement. Rather it now seemed to be concentrating its efforts upon the introduction of certain practices and outward observances which had been either banished from the Church of England at the Reformation or (though many of their advocates were not sufficient scholars to realize this) newly introduced into the Roman Catholic Church since the Council of Trent (1545–63).*

One of these was the practice of private confession. It had never completely ceased in the Church of England since the Reformation. The Prayer Book urged its use in cases of uneasy conscience or sickness, and no doubt people had always sought the confidential advice of a clergyman when in anxiety or distress; but the idea of confession regularly practised as an obligation was a different matter. This had fallen into disuse and was generally regarded as a piece of priestly pretension to power. Newman had said at Oxford in 1842:

> As to reminding my people about Confession, it is the most dreary and dismal thought I have about my parish, that I dare so little, or rather nothing. I have long thought it would hinder me from ever taking another cure. Confession is the life of the parochial charge; without it all is hollow, and yet I do not see my way to say that I should not do more harm than good by more than the most distant mention of it. Reading the first Exhortation at the Communion is the only thing I do of a direct kind. I hope that it is of a nature to startle those who listen, though not enough perhaps to persuade them.
>
> Anne Mozley (ed), *Letters and Correspondence of J. H. Newman during his Life in the English Church* (2 vols, 1891), II, 405.

Newman's friends, however, persisted in reviving private confession. Pusey became a noted confessor at Oxford, and so did Keble in his country parish of Hursley, near Winchester, of which he was Vicar for the last thirty years of his life. Opposition to it, however, remained very strong. Lord Shaftesbury continually urged the bishops to declare it illegal. This they would not do, and when the Lambeth Conference* of 1878 issued a declaration on the subject, it did so in terms which insisted that the Church of England regarded it as a voluntary means of helping the individual towards the attainment of the Christian life, available if he wished to resort to it, but not to be erected into a comprehensive system of compulsory discipline. After mentioning the two cases in which the Prayer Book made provision for confession, the declaration went on to say:

> This special provision, however, does not authorise the Ministers of the Church to require, from any who may resort to them to open their grief, a particular or detailed enumeration of all their sins, or to require private Confession previous to receiving the 'Holy Communion,' or to enjoin or even encourage any practice of habitual Confession to a priest, or to teach that such practice of habitual Confession, or the being subject to what has been termed the direction of a priest, is a condition of attaining to the highest spiritual life.

R. T. Davidson & W. Benham, *Life of Archbishop Tait* (2 vols, 1891), II, 170.

There were, however, clergymen whose use of confession was according to the Roman method rather than the Anglican, and the matter continued to excite spasmodic controversy for the rest of the century; but as a subject of contention it was outpaced by what came to be known as 'ritualism'. This expressed the desire of later Tractarians to make the worship of the Church of England more reverent and inspiring, a desire which was not confined to them alone; it had been the aim of many Evangelical clergymen previously. The Reformation changed the focus of worship in the parish churches from the altar to the pulpit, and the rationalism and lack of spirituality of the eighteenth century had further converted many churches into well-pewed preaching houses in which worship and the sacraments seemed almost crowded out. This is a description of a not-untypical instance from the Cornish countryside, the Church of St Finbarras, Fowey, in the late 1820s:

> I can remember the grand old church to which I was taken every Sunday, and the great square pew in which I was boxed up, and the seats all round from which the family circle looked at each other, or, when they knelt, turned their backs on each other. The whole church was fitted with pews of a similar character. I remember the parson's desk, and the clerk's desk, and their alternate reading of the verses of the Psalms, in which very few of the congregation ever joined, for the clerk's responses, though in a monotone, were not musical or easy to join in. The altar was blocked out of sight altogether by the high square pews, but the Holy Communion was celebrated there once a month, I was told.

> There was a high gallery at the west end of the nave, which was reached by a steep flight of stairs, and to this gallery, which had the Royal Arms in front, the clerk went to give out some verses of one of the metrical Psalms composed by Messrs. Tate and Brady. Hymns of any kind were not considered orthodox or correct in those days. The aged vicar then went to the pulpit in a black gown and read a sermon, and so the service ended. It was certainly not a lively function and was not calculated to aid the devotions of the congregation . . .
>
> A. Clifton Kelway, *George Rundle Prynne* (1905), 6–7.

Newman himself revived the use of the chancel in St Mary's when he started a daily morning service there in 1834. He said it from a desk he had put up near the altar. He made no attempt, however, to depart from the externals of worship as they commonly existed in his time. Throughout his ministry in the Church of England he celebrated Holy Communion at the 'north end' of the altar and wore a surplice and academic hood. And so did Pusey and the other Tractarians. They were concerned with invisible, not visible, things and were indifferent or even hostile to those who wished to revive old, disused practices in the conduct of the services. When Pusey wrote in 1839 to J. F. Russell, Vicar of St Peter's, Walworth, he said that he feared that concern with ritual on the part of the clergy could lead to vanity and individualism:

> On this ground among others, I should deprecate seeking to restore the richer style of vestments used in Edward the Sixth's reign . . . It seems beginning at the wrong end for the ministers to deck their own persons: our own plain dresses are more in keeping with the state of our Church, which is one of humiliation: it does not seem in character to revive gorgeous or even in any degree handsome dresses in a day of reproach and rebuke and blasphemy: these are not holyday times.
>
> H. P. Liddon, *op cit*, II, 142.

The restraint of the old Tractarians, however, was not shared by the new generation of Anglo-Catholics, and the revival of ceremonial soon became a feature of the movement. It was, in fact, begun at Littlemore by Newman's curate, John Rouse Bloxam (1807–91), who introduced into the church there various ornaments, among them gilded candlesticks, a credence table, a litany desk, a wooden alms-dish and a black silk stole. Soon afterwards these innovations were copied by Frederick Oakley (1802–80), who from 1839 to 1845 was in charge of the Margaret Chapel, London (on the site of the present All Saints' Church, Margaret Street), which became a centre of Tractarian worship. Oakley followed Newman into the Roman Catholic Church, but under his successors the ceremonial developments at the church went further. In

Margaret Chapel, 1845

The last celebration of the Feast of the Epiphany at Margaret Chapel, 1850

1847, Benjamin Webb, Vicar of St Andrew's, Wells Street, London, wrote to John Mason Neale (1818–66), Warden of Sackville College, East Grinstead, Sussex, who had introduced the same ornaments as well as coloured altar-frontals into the chapel of this almshouse:

> At Margaret Chapel they have now got up a complete musical Mass: the Commandments, Epistle, Gospel, Preface, etc, all sung to the ancient music. I wish you would take a day-ticket for the Epiphany, . . . there has been nothing so solemn since the Reformation.
>
> Mary S. Lawson (ed), *Letters of John Mason Neale* (1910), 107.

The first Tractarian movement had been centred upon Oxford; the Ritualist movement owed more to Cambridge. Neale was one of the founders of the Cambridge Camden Society in 1839, which stimulated interest in Church architecture and traditional Catholic worship. In the space of a generation the movement developed apace until there were churches in which the services were conducted in a manner that marked them apart from the rest. One of these was St Barnabas, Oxford, visited by Francis Kilvert, who was then Curate at Langley Burrell, Wiltshire, and was in Oxford on Ascension Day, 1876:

We went to hear Father Stanton preach at St Barnabas. The service was at 8 o'clock and the evening light was setting behind the lofty Campanile as we entered. The large Church was almost full, the great congregation singing like one man. The clergy and choir entered with a procession, incense bearers and a great gilt cross, the thurifers and acolytes being in short white surplices over scarlet cassocks and the last priest in the procession wearing a biretta and a chasuble stiff with gold. The Magnificat seemed to be the central point in the service and at the words 'For behold from henceforth all generations shall call me blessed' the black biretta and golden chasuble (named Shuttleworth) advanced, was 'censed' by the thurifer, then took the censer from him and censed the cross, the banners, the lights and the altar, till the Church was all in a fume. At least so Mayhew said. I myself could not see exactly what was done though I knew some ceremony was going on. It appeared to me to be pure Mariolatry. Father Stanton took for his text 'He is altogether lovely', Canticles ii. The matter was not original or interesting, and the manner was theatrical and overdone. I should think every eye in that great congregation was quite dry. The text was repeated constantly in a very low die-away tone. The sermon came after the Third Collect. I was disappointed in it and so I think were many more. After the service there was an offertory and a processional hymn, and then round came the procession down the South aisle and up the nave in the following order. First the thurifer in short white surplice and scarlet cassock swinging a chained censer high in the air and bringing it back with a sudden check and violent jerk which brought the incense out in stifling cloud. Next an acolyte in a similar dress bearing aloft a great gilt cross. Then three banners waving and moving above the heads of the people in a weird strange ghostly march, as the banner-bearers steered them clear of the gaslights. After them came two wand-bearers preceding the clergy, Father Stanton walking in the midst and looking exhausted, the rear of the procession being brought up by the hideous figure of the emaciated ghost in the black biretta and golden chasuble.

As we came out of Church Mayhew said to me, '*Well*, did you ever see such a function as that?' No, I never did and I don't care if I never do again. This was the grand function of the Ascension at St Barnabas, Oxford. The poor humble Roman Church hard by is quite plain, simple and Low Church in its ritual compared with St Barnabas in its festal dress on high days and holidays.

Francis Kilvert, *Diary*, 25th May 1876.

As the ritualistic movement progressed, many of its protagonists adopted ideals which were practically those of the modern Roman Catholic Church. Clerical trippers, who were ignorant of the usage of the pre-Reformation English Church, made visits to the Continent and came back resolved to introduce into their own churches the ceremonies they had seen. Soon it was not uncommon to find churches in which the Prayer Book service of Holy Communion was celebrated as if it were the Roman Mass. The impression this development made upon Matthew Arnold was similar to that made on many people:

> Who that watches the energumens during the celebration of the Communion in some Ritualistic church, the gestures and behaviour, the floor of the church strewn with what seem to be the dying and the dead, progress to the altar almost barred by forms suddenly dropping as if they were shot in battle,—who that observes this delighted adoption of vehement rites, till yesterday unknown, adopted and practised now with all that absence of tact, measure, and correct perception in things of form and manner, all that slowness to see when they are making themselves ridiculous, which belongs to the people of our English race,—who, I say, that marks this can doubt, that for a not small portion of our religious community a difficulty to the intelligence will for a long time yet be no difficulty at all? With their mental condition and habits, given a story to which their religious emotions can attach themselves, and the famous *Credo quia ineptum* will hold good with them still. To think they know what passed in the Council of the Trinity is not hard to them; they could easily think they even knew what were the hangings of the Trinity's council-chamber.
>
> Matthew Arnold, *Literature and Dogma* (1873), chap. ix.

Matthew Arnold's attitude was that of most educated men of the time. If the Evangelicals had failed to get the support of such people, the Ritualists certainly did not. And they came into contact with public opinion more dramatically than the Evangelicals ever had. Outwardly they were extreme innovators. They had a conception of worship which was markedly different from that familiar to Englishmen for generations, and congregations are notoriously conservative in their attitude towards the way in which services are conducted. Moreover, ritualism spread in the Church of England at the time when the growing strength of Roman Catholicism was causing concern and resentment in the country, and the Ritualists appeared to be encouraging it from within. Consequently there was rioting and scenes of violence at ritualistic churches and a growing demand that something should be done to suppress what was alleged to be an unlawful movement. The result was the Public Worship Regulation Act of 1874, which was introduced in the House of Lords by the Archbishop of Canterbury, Dr A. C. Tait, and passed through Parliament with the support of Lord

Shaftesbury and Benjamin Disraeli. It was passionately opposed by W. E. Gladstone, who wrote a memorandum on it at the time:

> The changes effected during the present year were probably proposed with the belief that they would be agreeable to a majority, and that this majority, when better contented with its position, would exert itself more harmoniously and more efficaciously to maintain the political establishment of the Church.
>
> But this plausible reasoning was full of flaws; and probably the promoters of the recent Bill were little aware what responsibility they were loading upon themselves. They committed, in the first place, the same great error as was committed by the projectors of the Scottish Church Patronage Bill: they assumed that they had only to do with those who were within the Church, and forgot those who were without. They not only forgot that many would concur in their proposals with the purpose of working them for purposes which they disapprove, but satisfied with counting their numbers for the first encounter, they did not ask themselves how they would stand when many of their friends would become opponents, and none of their opponents would become friends. They forgot that in this country and in this age, outside of all sects and ecclesiastical parties, there exists a great floating mass of those who do not so value any of the religious alternatives proposed to them, as to prefer them to a quiet life. They forgot that there is many an ancient fabric not too old or weak to stand, but too old for ambitious or organic repair.
>
> D. C. Lathbury (ed), *Correspondence on Church and Religion of William Ewart Gladstone* (2 vols, 1910), I, 393.

Gladstone was right in supposing that the Act would not achieve its object. Despite the indifference of the bishops and the general hostility of the laity, Anglo-Catholicism gained growing support from the lower clergy, including many of the ablest. At a time when the Church had been deprived of most of its legal privileges, this movement, which insisted that salvation must be obtained through the grace of sacraments administered by episcopally ordained priests, renewed their importance. Yet the opponents of the movement made what use they could of the Act. In 1880 alone the incumbents of five parishes were prosecuted under it for 'ritualistic offences', and one was sent to prison. These prosecutions, however, were far from destroying the movement, and in 1881 Lord Salisbury, the Conservative leader, wrote to Tait:

> In these 'congregational' churches, where the congregation and the incumbent are agreed, I think the Bishops would do wisely to shield the incumbent from

litigation, at least if he did not go further than to act upon the apparently literal interpretation of the Ornaments Rubric. If this were accorded and announced, I do not believe that the incumbents of the older churches would attempt similar practices in opposition to the feelings of their parishioners . . . Ritualism is too strong to be 'put down'; a serious attempt to do so would simply shatter the Church. On the other hand, it is odious to the majority of Churchmen, partly from habit, partly from dogmatic conviction. The time is passed by when it was possible to conciliate these rival bodies of opinion. If a fatal collision is to be avoided the only thing to be done is to get them into different buildings. If the Bishops could be induced to take this view, they might do much to bring about such a distribution of worshippers by a judicious and systematic exercise of their veto on legislation.

R. T. Davidson & W. Benham, *op cit*, II, 449.

In 1885 Gladstone appointed Dr Edward King to the bishopric of Lincoln. Though not extreme, King was more of a Ritualist than any bishop so far approved by Queen Victoria; and late in 1888 the Church Association, a Protestant organization, arraigned him for illegal practices in divine worship before the Archbishop of Canterbury, Dr E. W. Benson. He heard the case in 1890, assisted by five bishops with the intention of avoiding such a scandal as had been caused by the Gorham Case (see p. 71). The Archbishop's judgment upheld King on most of the points, which included altar lights, the mixed chalice and the eastward position taken by the priest when celebrating at the altar. The Church Association appealed in 1892 to the Privy Council, which refused to upset the judgment. Many suspected that Benson's intention was to shield the Ritualists and so prevent an open conflict within the Church. Lord Robert Montagu in a pamphlet, *The Lambeth Judgment; or the Masks of Sacerdotalism* (1891), candidly stated what he supposed to be Benson's actual motive:

A peculiar but well-defined character runs through the Judgment, as subsidiary to the primary aim of judging certain ritualistic acts. The former is veiled and hidden; the latter is open and avowed. I mean that there can be traced a continued endeavour to defend Romish symbols, and the Romish doctrines which are inculcated by those symbols, and especially the doctrine of transubstantiation; although the outward appearance of shunning all approaches to popery is throughout carefully maintained—so much so, that in two or three instances the practice of the Church of Rome has been so incorrectly stated, that the High Church imitation of it does not appear to be popish . . .

E. R. Norman, *Anti-Catholicism in Victorian England* (1968), 234–5.

Benson was certainly a man of peace and probably sympathized more with the Ritualists than he cared to admit in public; and, whatever his motives, his judgment was a considerable victory for the Ritualists. Moderate opinion, already upset by the imprisonment of clergymen, was scandalized by the trial of a bishop, particularly because King was known for his saintly character. The opponents of ritualism had to abandon their attempts to crush it, and its practices continued to spread in the parish churches for the rest of the century. Still more, its influence raised the level of worship in churches other than those which could be regarded as ritualistic. This was shown in the changes made in St Paul's Cathedral by Robert Gregory, who became a Canon in 1868 and the Dean in 1890, and rescued it from a condition similar to that which Trollope had described in Westminster Abbey. The results of the changes were summed up in the *Guardian* in March 1878:

> How great that work is can only be appreciated by those who remember what the Cathedral was a score of years ago, when you paid twopence at the door to enter a vast and dreary area abandoned to dust and damp and uselessness. All that has long ago been altered. No one feels now the chill of an unused building as he enters unquestioned the long aisles abundantly fitted up for Worship. Even the vast Crypt, formerly a mere lumberhole, is being gradually cleared out, and a portion of it is already used for some of the many Services which, in the various demands made and accepted on the Metropolitan Cathedral, are occasionally jostling one another; and if the renovation of the whole fabric is still delayed, it is rather from a wholesome desire to wait for the final award of a deliberate taste and judgment in so important a matter, than from a lack of enterprise or despair of funds. Meanwhile, that which is really the life of the Church goes on with unremitting, and indeed ever-increasing vigour . . . The nation and the City both look to it as the conspicuous embodiment of their visible Worship, the bond of their united religious activities, the heart which sends the pulse of Religion bounding actively through a thousand different channels. It has borne a striking witness to the power which may flow from a great ecclesiastical institution rightly planned and diligently and wisely worked in the midst of a teeming and busy population.
>
> S. C. Carpenter, *op cit*, 294–5.

6 The Sisterhoods and the Slums

A notable consequence of the Tractarian movement was the revival of the monastic ideal within the Church of England for the first time since the destruction of the abbeys in the sixteenth century. This was an astonishing achievement, but it was a development inherent in the outlook of the early Tractarians. Like the first Methodists at Oxford in the previous century, who had drawn upon themselves the nickname of the 'Holy Club', they devoted themselves to the ideal of personal holiness, but they also cast it in a romantically medieval form. Pusey, Hurrell Froude and Newman upheld the sanctity of the celibate life. Newman, indeed, seems to have had an almost pathological dislike of the idea of marriage. This is revealed in the passage in his novel, *Loss and Gain*, describing how his young hero, Charles Reding, shortly before his reception into the Roman Catholic Church, was in a book-shop and heard the door open:

> On looking round, he saw a familiar face. It was that of a young clergyman, with a very pretty girl on his arm, whom her dress pronounced to be a bride. Love was in their eyes, joy in their voice and affluence in their gait and bearing. Charles had a faintish feeling come over him; somewhat such as might beset a man on hearing a call for pork-chops when he was seasick. He remained behind a pile of ledgers and other stationery, but they could not save him from the low, dulcet tones which from time to time passed from one to the other.
>
> J. H. Newman, *Loss and Gain* (1848), 349.

Newman's departure to Littlemore with a company of young disciples during his final Anglican years was entirely consistent with his character. There, in stables partitioned into six sets of small rooms, the small community devoted itself to study and prayer, saying the old daily monastic services. The dominating idea of this revival of monasticism was that of peace and meditation and retreat from the world; but the wider Anglican revival was to have a different emphasis. In it women played the most important part and were strongly influenced by the pastoral motive. English travellers abroad were impressed by the sight of Roman Catholic nuns in hospitals and prisons, orphanages and slums, while in several places in England there were now convents established by the members of French orders who had fled during the French Revolution. In December 1825 a Dr Gooch, writing in *Blackwood's Magazine* about the hospital work of the Béguines in Belgium, said:

> Let the Church, or if not, let that class of Christians in whom, above all others, religion is not a mere Sunday ceremony, but the daily and hourly principle of their thoughts and actions, and of whom I have only to complain for a little error in doctrine, and more than a little cant at least in language, which latter peculiarity is perpetually preventing the success of their religious appeals, at least to educated minds, and which is as great an obstacle to the first steps in religion as technical jargon to the first steps in science—let all serious Christians, I say, join and found an order of women like the Sisters of Charity in Catholic countries; let them be selected for good plain sense, kindness of disposition, indefatigable industry, and deep piety; let them receive not a technical and scientific, but a practical medical education; for this purpose, let them be placed as nurses and pupils in the hospitals of Edinburgh or London, or in the country hospitals.
>
> P. F. Anson, *The Call of the Cloister* (1955), 25–6.

The first Anglican sisterhood, the Sisterhood of the Holy Cross, was founded in 1845 at Park Village West, near Regent's Park in London, by Lord John Manners, with the help of Dodsworth, Pusey, Hook and Gladstone, as a memorial to Robert Southey, the Poet Laureate, who had urged the revival of sisterhoods in the Church. It began as a community of eight ladies, who taught in a school for pauper children, conducted an orphanage and visited the slums off the Euston Road. One of these Sisters has given a vivid picture of the usual routine they followed:

> The Sisters rose at five o'clock, or at least were supposed to do so, for several were unable as well as myself. The service called *Lauds* was then said in the Oratory ... At a quarter to seven o'clock, the orphans and Sisters assembled in the same room, and *Prime* was said. Breakfast followed, which was taken in silence; indeed, silence was observed all day, except at the hours appointed for recreation. After that meal we said *Terce*, and went to hear morning prayers read in the church ... The Sisters who taught in the poor school went then to their duties, and the Sisters who had charge of the orphans to theirs ... The poor children were taken to church also. After prayers, on their return to the schoolroom, they were provided with a good meal of rice and milk. In order to ensure their exterior attention to the service, which very few of them were old enough to

understand, a rule was made that every child who misbehaved should get no sugar. The rule worked admirably.

The school lasted until twelve, when we returned home, and said *Sext.* We had dinner at twenty minutes after one, still in silence; the food was plain, good and sufficient. After dinner we talked together in the 'common-room', or what in a convent would be called the community room. At three we said *None.* The Sisters appointed to attend the school, if I remember correctly, omitted the service altogether. The school was dismissed for the day at half-past four. At five there were three quarters of an hour for spiritual reading, then *Vespers.* Supper followed at six, and after it a few minutes recreation. We then prepared for church, and those who could not go, after the fatigues of the day, read the service at home. On our return from church, at eight o'clock *Compline* was read, and the Sisters remained in the Oratory after its conclusion for private devotion until twenty minutes past nine, when *Matins* was said. At ten all were supposed to be in bed.

Margaret Cusack, *Five Years in a Protestant Sisterhood* (1869), 23–5.

In 1848 W. J. Butler, then Vicar of Wantage, established the Community of St Mary the Virgin, which founded a school and a home for unmarried mothers. And in the same year, with Pusey's encouragement, Priscilla Lydia Sellon (1821–76) established the Society of the Holy Trinity at Devonport, where they soon had an orphanage, a home for delinquent boys, a refuge to train girls for domestic service, a home for old sailors, a school to teach seventy girls needlework, five ragged schools, six model lodging-houses with a school attached, and a soup kitchen serving over eighty meals daily to paupers too old to work. The year after the establishment of the community, the cholera broke out in Plymouth and raged especially in the poor parish of St Peter. The Vicar, G. R. Prynne, accepted Miss Sellon's offer of help from her Sisters, and at her urgent request several Sisters from the Park Village community came to join them as long as the outbreak lasted. The Vicar has described that terrible time:

For three months we seemed to be living amongst the dying and the dead. A large wooden hospital for the whole of Plymouth was erected in our parish. We set up an altar in the largest ward, in order that everything might always be ready for communicating the dying. As the visitation reached its climax the deaths became very frequent and rapid . . . It was during the raging of the cholera that the Sisters asked to be allowed to receive Holy Communion daily to strengthen them for their daily work.

A. Clifton Kelway, *op cit*, 50–4.

This was the first institution of a daily celebration in the Church of England, and it was continued after the cholera epidemic was over, being transferred from the altar in the cholera hospital to St Peter's Church. Indeed, from the first the new sisterhoods took an important part in the ritualistic movement, particularly in the development of devotions centred upon the sacrament of the altar. The chapels of these convents were private places of worship and not subject, therefore, to the same episcopal control or public criticism as parish churches and cathedrals. Thus, St Margaret's Convent, East Grinstead, founded by Neale in 1855, was the first Anglican place of worship to introduce the practice of continuous Reservation.*

Neale, however, not only possessed an interest in liturgical details. He was also moved by a deep concern for the wretched conditions under which many of the poor people lived in the countryside around East Grinstead. Social historians have tended to concentrate upon the miseries of the urban, industrial working-class in the nineteenth century, but the plight of many rural labourers and their families was often no less serious:

> Below the town lies a green belt of pasture-land, beyond which the great brown ridges of Ashdown Forest sweep the southern horizon . . . Away eastward, a richly-wooded green country stretches away till it melts into the blue distances of Reigate and Dorking. Beautiful as this lovely view is to look at, scattered over the vast area, buried in the woods and wilds, were innumerable hamlets and isolated cottages, badly built, badly drained, far from human help and resource, when fever or any illness attacked the inmates. Day after day, as he paced, as his custom was, up and down this terrace, and looked out over the fair scene, his heart burned within him at the thought of all the miseries of these wretched cottages . . . Scholar, student, poetically imaginative man though he was, he was not one to simply sigh and sympathize, and then let things take their course. He no sooner felt an existent evil than he tried to find a remedy for it. And so it came to pass that God put it into his heart to try to form a Sisterhood, whose special object should be to try to go out into these poor cottages, to live with, and nurse the sufferers under their own roof. It seemed a wild idea, a hopelessly impracticable one. People were stiffer, and more set in their own special grooves than now-a-days, and society was more aghast at any departure from routine. Besides the Bishop had inhibited him for having a Bible with a cross on the cover, and a cross and candlesticks on the Communion Table.
>
> Mother Kate, *Memories of a Sister of St Saviour's Priory* (1912), 13–15.

These were the recollections of an early member of this Society of St Margaret which met with considerable opposition in its early days. When the first five Sisters moved into a small eighteenth-century house in East Grinstead, the Vicar preached a sermon in the parish church on the dangers of Popery. Then, Neale recounted:

> Miss Gream [the first Mother Superior of the Society] called on him, to explain to him, that in coming here they had not the remotest intention of interfering with him or his parish; though, of course, if he liked to employ them, etc. He was quite as civil as could be expected; said that he knew the great benefit of good nursing, etc, but that if ever he asked them to nurse, they must expect to have their religious practices looked very carefully after.
>
> Mary S. Lawson, *Letters of John Mason Neale* (1910), 272.

Episcopal approval was equally difficult to obtain. Bishop Gilbert of Chichester inhibited Neale in 1847 because of his 'spiritual haberdashery', and Neale was unable to officiate in the chapel of Sackville College until 1860. Bishop Gilbert, who was an old-fashioned high churchman, at first welcomed the Sisterhood, but withdrew his patronage in 1857 after a riot in Lewes at the funeral of a Sister whose father alleged that the Society had forced her to make a will in its favour. Gilbert's successor in 1870 was Richard Durnford, whose ecclesiastical outlook was very similar. He asked the Sisterhood to discontinue Reservation. They 'positively refused to do so', though they did change the place of Reservation from the convent chapel to an adjoining room. Durnford considered Reservation* an unnecessary and superstitious practice:

> The sisters communicate daily, and the Holy Sacrament ought to be administered to any of them at a very short warning. It seems to countenance a material presence of our Blessed Lord, independent of the act of communion, in the elements themselves ... I on my part most reluctantly found myself unable to give them that full countenance which I should have desired to give to a body whose good works are so conspicuous and whose purpose and life are, I doubt not, holy ... So many things in their rules and in their words—e.g. the name of the *convent*—studiously used, show an approximation to Rome which is hardly safe, and which provokes needless opposition and suspicion.
>
> W. R. W. Stephens, *Memoir of Richard Durnford* (1899), 245–6.

By then, however, the Society had gone on from strength to strength. It had established an orphanage and a school for girls at East Grinstead; in 1865, a year before Neale's death, the foundation stone of the present St Margaret's Convent had

The Chapel, Sackville College, East Grinstead

been laid, and the Society possessed what were then the most magnificent conventual buildings in England. By then, also, the community had begun to work in the slums of London, at first in Soho and later in Haggerston where it established St Saviour's Priory as a branch house. Early in the twentieth century Charles Booth paid a tribute to the work carried on by the Sisters there, though he considered that they achieved very little result indeed:

> Of these Sisters twenty-eight live here and work in four of the adjacent parishes. Thirteen are allocated to St Augustine's, and these are, to a great extent, responsible for the parish organization. The Priory itself is the centre for a number of charitable operations. There is a dispensary at which doctors' prescriptions are made up for the bare cost of the drugs, and simple remedies are given away. There are halfpenny dinners for the schoolchildren and, in winter, free dinners for men out of work and occasional free teas on Sundays. Dinners are also sent out to the sick, and thousands of tickets for bread and groceries or

coals are given away. Work is found for women. Immense quantities of old clothes are collected and sold at nominal prices, together with new garments specially made and sent for this purpose; contributions being acknowledged from no fewer than two hundred 'local centres' or other sources.

Charles Booth, *Life and Labour of the People of London* (1902: Third Series, Religious Influences, vol II), 89–92.

This part of London, where the Sisters devoted themselves to these charitable activities which afford a grim insight into the lives of the poor, had been called by then 'the most extensive and closely concentrated Anglo-Catholic outpost in the whole of London', the convent being the centre of a group of parishes where the clergy shared its outlook; and, indeed, when Tractarianism began to spread from Oxford out into the country, it was into slum parishes that many of its clerical followers went. The same pastoral ideals, which inspired the sisterhoods and their founders, animated these young clergymen. If Anglo-Catholicism was to gain the country, it must be a missionary movement, and it could not do better than begin its work among the poor in the large towns, whose material circumstances were pitiable and whose spiritual condition was alarming. There now came into being a class of parochial clergymen who concerned themselves with the most wretched of their parishioners in a way hardly known before. In the summer of 1868, for instance, George Howard Wilkinson, later to become Bishop of Truro, began street-preaching. He had come from Bishop Auckland in County Durham to be Vicar of St Peter's, Great Windmill Street, near to London's Piccadilly Circus, a parish in which there was a mixture of gay amusement and degradation and misery. On the first occasion he halted to preach at the top of Rupert Street. The occasion was diligently described by his children's governess:

Mr Wilkinson in surplice and hood, supported by his curates and followed by choir and churchwardens, walked in procession from the church singing hymns. Such a spectacle seemed so odd in those squalid London streets. Arrived at the place chosen for the sermon, or rather address, as I should call it, we were glad to see a good many of the class we wanted gathered together, besides some of the better people who attend the church. Mr W. preached with great power. It was a tremendous exertion, but his voice was distinctly heard to the very edge of the crowd. He told them that he had given up much in leaving the North to come among them, and how he longed for their souls, picturing to them the life so many of them had been living, and their sore need of a Saviour. A good many listened most attentively, and accepted his invitation to follow him into church for some prayer. It was indeed such a singular scene—the tall houses with

> hideous-looking women hanging out of every window, dirty men with short pipes in their mouths, the tawdry-fine work-girl, the jaunty shop boy, the city arab, the fat, prosperous-looking landlady in silk and velvet, a man selling apples and ginger beer, with a soldier or two, and rising up in the midst Mr Wilkinson's refined, thoughtful face and pure white surplice.
>
> A. J. Mason, *Memoir of George Howard Wilkinson* (1910), 102.

In parishes where the inhabitants belonged with almost unbroken uniformity to the poorest of the poor, the clergymen who came to live and work among them were often greeted at first with hostility, which gradually changed to friendliness. The incumbent of a slum parish was generally the only professional man residing there, the only man capable of giving leadership, help and advice. When riots occurred against ritualistic services, as in St George's-in-the-East in 1859 and 1860, they were usually the work of criminals and roughs. Many a priest in a poor parish gathered around him a congregation who were attracted by his ministrations.

This had been done as early as 1845 by G. A. Skinner, who was curate in charge of St Barnabas', Pimlico, then a daughter church of St Paul's, Knightsbridge. His church was in a particularly degraded part of the parish. An open sewer ran through it into the Thames, and it had a largely criminal population. Skinner wrote:

> Bishop Blomfield had stopped in great manner the choral worship at St Paul's, and he had ordered it to be stopped at St Barnabas. I honestly tried to obey him, but my first attempt at 'saying' instead of 'singing' the versicles was received by the congregation with so loud and determined a burst of song in the responses, that I felt obliged to go to the Bishop, and to tell him plainly that, if choral service was to be discontinued at St Barnabas', I must decline to have any responsibility for keeping order there. The people were *determined* to assert and use the liberty given in the Prayer Book. I told him so distinctly, and the Bishop did not persevere.
>
> Maria Trench, *Charles Lowder: A Biography* (1881), 30.

Indeed, the ritualistic clergyman found that he had a freedom which would have been denied him if he had been the incumbent of a long-established, well-attended suburban church or a country parish dominated by a powerful squire. It became increasingly common for bishops who attempted to prohibit ritualistic services in churches in working-class parishes to meet with opposition from members of the congregation. Thirty years after Bishop Blomfield's experience with St Barnabas', Pimlico, John Jackson, an Evangelical who had succeeded Tait as Bishop of London, sought to check the ritualistic practices of A. H. Mackonochie, the Vicar of the newly built St Alban's Church, Holborn, in a parish which contained some of the worst streets and alleys of London. The parishioners and members of the congregation sent him this petition:

> The ritual that has been gradually developed has been requested at each successive stage by the laity, so that there is no pretence for saying that it has been forced upon an unwilling congregation . . . We firmly believe in all the doctrines of which ritual is but the outward sign. We value lights, incense and kneeling, because they teach the Real Presence of our Blessed Lord in the Holy Eucharist. We lament the removal of the Crucifix because it so eloquently preached Christ crucified. And we regret the removal of the Confessionals, which has been caused by an interference which is inconsistent with religious liberty. We feel that if the opposition be honest, it is aimed rather at doctrine than at ritual; so that while we have the plain words of the Prayer Book to teach us the former, we claim the right of having the latter to set it forth more clearly. We further believe that the ritual used is entirely in accordance with the law of the Church of England, and with the spirit of the Prayer Book, which cannot be interpreted by the neglect of past years, and upon which the conflicting judgments in recent suits throw no light whatever . . . This question touches the laity very deeply . . . There are thousands of members of the Church of England who feel as we do . . . We declare our unfeigned devotion to our branch of the Catholic Church. We beg your Lordship to remember that the Church of England has under its present constitution always embraced men of various schools of thought. And we venture to leave in your Lordship's hands this our strongest possible protest, desiring only that liberty and toleration which is extended to all other schools in the Church.
>
> Eleanor Towle, *Alexander Heriot Mackonochie: A Memoir* (1890), 161.

As the century progressed, newly ordained Anglo-Catholic curates (and a growing number of such curates were Anglo-Catholics) were strongly attracted to work in slum parishes. There was great freedom of action for them there, but there was also opposition and hard work which called for heroic qualities, together with a sense that they really were doing good and working among people who needed their ministry. Compared with their clerical fellows in more respectable and wealthy parishes, they might hope to lead considerably more useful and eventful lives. An example of such a parish priest was Robert Dolling ('Father Dolling'), who from 1885 to 1896 was in charge of St Agatha's, Landport, the Winchester College Mission in Portsmouth, where he fought very successfully against the evils of slum life and achieved a remarkable transformation in the parish through his influence. Next to the mission was a brothel, the patrons of which mistakenly knocked him up at all hours of the night. Its proprietoress (whom he later bought out) interrupted his services, including the dedication of the new parsonage in 1889:

> A procession of choir, acolytes and priests was moving from room to room with lighted candles and clouds of incense. At the end came Father Dolling, in a gorgeous cope, saying the office of benediction for each part of the building, the crowded congregation meanwhile filling up all the vacant spaces in the house and the gymnasium. In the intervals of the devotions raucous shrieks were heard proceeding from the harridan who was responsible for the house next door, and who in its back-yard was heard invoking many curses both loud and deep upon the heads of 'old Dolling and his pack of Catholics'. Like the silversmiths of Ephesus, she felt, no doubt, that her gains were likely to be interfered with.
>
> C. E. Osborne, *Life of Father Dolling* (1903), 98.

By the 1870s such figures had become the new leaders of Anglo-Catholicism. The younger members of the movement no longer looked to the universities for their inspiration and example. For them the heroes of the Church were the parochial clergy working in the poorer parts of the capital, the industrial towns and the ports. They now claimed that such men were the backbone of the movement and that the bishops were risking disaster for the Church by harrying them. In 1870 Mackonochie himself wrote to the Evangelical periodical, *The Record*, in which he claimed that the Anglo-Catholics were the true successors of the Methodists and the Evangelicals:

> Let me ask you, Sir: Who drove Wesley from the Church of England? The Bishops and the Upper Middle Classes in Church and State. In fact the 'Chief Priests with the Scribes and Pharisees'. Who are now trying to drive from the Church those who are the fruits of the labour of Wesley and the old Evangelicals? The same 'Chief Priests with the Scribes and Pharisees'. An old and highly respected priest of the Evangelical section of the Church, lately gone happily to his rest, used to say, 'If you want to find an old Evangelical, you must look for him in the ranks of the extreme High Churchmen'.
>
> A. H. Mackonochie, *Letter Addressed to The Record* (1870), 13.

It was true that the Anglo-Catholics made up the most active and rapidly growing movement in the Church and that devoted work was being done by both priests and sisters in many poor parishes, but nevertheless the movement had serious weaknesses.

There were more than a few churches in industrial districts with big congregations, which contained, however, few of the poor people of the parish and a good many who had come from a distance, attracted by the ritualistic services. And such people were a minority in the Church. The great majority of lay people angrily repudiated the ritualistic services. In most parishes their indignation was intense when the sung Mass, done after Anglo-Catholic fashion, replaced the traditional Matins and sermon on Sundays. Such a protest as this, though couched in typically Victorian style, represented a genuine grievance which told against the Anglo-Catholics' ever gaining universal acceptance in the Church:

> I have now lived in this parish for ten years, and although a churchman by birth and conviction, I and my family are utterly unable to attend the parish church owing to the practises which are carried on there . . . There are persons of high position living in the parish, who, like myself, are prevented from attending their parish church, and a great number of villagers in this large parish refuse to attend the parish church for a similar reason. There is a Roman Catholic chapel in which I understand the services are of a less extreme character than in the Protestant parish church.

Darwell Stone, *The Christian Church* (1905), 21, iv.

7 The Roman Catholics

At the same time as Tractarianism, Ritualism and Anglo-Catholicism were making progress in the Church of England, the Roman Catholics were becoming stronger and more assertive; and these two developments were often associated in the public mind. By 1815 they had benefited from the emigration to England from France of thousands of Roman Catholics, including priests, monks and nuns, who had fled from the persecution of the Revolution. Nevertheless, the Roman Catholics then were a very small minority in England, forming perhaps one or two per cent of the population. Their numbers had been greatly depleted through the effect of the penal laws, their attachment to the Jacobite cause, and secessions to the Church of England. In his sermon on 'The Second Spring', Newman described their position at the beginning of this period:

> No longer the Catholic Church in the country; nay, no longer, I may say, a Catholic community—but a few adherents of the Old Religion, moving silently and sorrowfully about, as memorials of what had been. 'The Roman Catholics'—not a sect, not even an interest, as men conceived it—not a body, however small, representative of the Great Communion abroad—but a mere handful of individuals, who might be counted, like the pebbles and *detritus* of the great deluge, and who, forsooth, merely happened to retain a creed which, in its day indeed, was the profession of a Church. Here a set of poor Irishmen, coming and going at harvest time, or a colony of them lodged in a miserable corner of the vast metropolis. There, perhaps, an elderly person, seen walking in the streets, grave and solitary . . . An old-fashioned house of gloomy appearance, closed in with high walls, with an iron gate and yews, and the report attaching to it that 'Roman Catholics' lived there; but who they were, or what they did, or what was meant by calling them 'Roman Catholics', no one could tell—though it had an unpleasant sound, and told of form and superstition.

Quoted, A. R. Vidler, *The Church in an Age of Revolution* (Pelican History of the Church, vol V, 1961), 42–3.

The repeal of the Test* and Corporation* Acts in 1828 brought Roman Catholics considerable benefits, but they were still subject to political discrimination. In the next year, however, the Irish campaign led by Daniel O'Connell compelled Parliament to pass a relief measure which enabled Roman Catholics to sit in either House of Parliament and to hold military, judicial and administrative posts under the Crown. Liberal opinion had long supported the principle of Roman Catholic emancipation, but it caused great disquiet in Anglican minds. The attempt of Sydney Smith (1771–1845), the reforming Canon of St Paul's, to allay their fears in his 'Letters of Peter Plymley' was calculated to cause disquiet and chagrin among those whom he professed to help:

> If a rich young Catholic were in parliament, he would belong to White's and to Brooke's, would keep race-horses, would walk up and down Pall Mall, be exonerated of his ready money and his constitution, become as totally devoid of morality, honesty, knowledge and civility as Protestant loungers in Pall Mall and return home with a supreme contempt for Father O'Leary and Father O'Callaghan. I am astonished at the madness of the Catholic clergy in not perceiving that Catholic emancipation is Catholic infidelity; that to entangle their people in the intrigues of a Protestant parliament and a Protestant Court is to ensure the loss of every man of fashion and consequence in their community.
>
> Sydney Smith, *Works* (2 vols, 1859), II, 175.

That this did not take place after Roman Catholic emancipation was due to a number of reasons, one being the changing intellectual climate of early Victorian England. The Rationalism of Sydney Smith's age was giving place to the new Romanticism and Tractarianism. The reception of Newman and other Tractarians into the Church of Rome seemed miraculous to its members. Great things were hoped from it. The conversion of England to Roman Catholicism seemed to be at hand. Members of old-established Roman Catholic families and converts alike were impressed by the possibilities that lay ahead of them. At the end of 1845 a letter appeared in a Roman Catholic magazine, written by one who signed himself 'A Convert of Nine Years Standing', which expressed the feelings of the time:

> The movement is assuredly only in its commencement, but I cannot help feeling that we Catholics have too often shown ourselves unworthy of the great mercies which have been poured upon us. Surely these first fruits ought to urge us to greater fervour and diligence than we have hitherto exhibited. Above all, let us be instant in prayer for the conversion of our country. Recent events have

given a palpable token of the efficacy of prayer. Woe be to us if we do not persevere . . . We have gained a few: many more remain behind. Perhaps this may be to urge us to persevere in prayer. The harvest is ready: only a few ripe shocks have as yet been gathered. Let us join then one and all in daily and special supplication for this desirable object. Above all, let us not in our private prayers shrink from petitioning in favour of individuals by name. May I suggest one worthy of veneration and which I rarely have omitted; one that all must respect, all must wish well to—there is a want among the returned pilgrims without him which all must deplore. Reader, may I recommend to your good prayers by name—that of Dr Pusey?
Orthodox Journal (December 1854), 288.

The secession of Pusey would have been a great prize for the Church of Rome, a final assurance that the logical culmination of Tractarianism lay in membership of its fold, and the event was continually awaited. And before long it looked as if this might happen. In 1847 the Lord Chancellor presented the Revd G. C. Gorham to the vicarage of Brampford Speke in the diocese of Exeter; but Henry Phillpotts, the Bishop of Exeter, suspected his orthodoxy and after examining him declared him unsound on the doctrine of baptismal regeneration* and refused to institute him to the living. After a complicated lawsuit, Gorham appealed to the Judicial Committee of the Privy Council, newly formed to hear cases from the ecclesiastical courts, which declared his views consistent with the doctrines of the Church of England. As Phillpotts still refused to institute him, Gorham was eventually instituted by the Archbishop of Canterbury. The case brought several further secessions to the Church of Rome, but not that of Pusey and other Tractarian leaders who supported Phillpotts, though they thought his action ill-advised. One of the fresh Roman converts, William Dodsworth (formerly of the Margaret Chapel), chided Pusey in an open letter:

By your constant and common practice of administering the sacrament of penance; by encouraging everywhere, if not enjoining, auricular confession; and giving special priestly absolution; by teaching the propitiary sacrifice of the Holy Eucharist, as applicatory of the one sacrifice on the Cross, and by an adoration of Christ Really Present on the Altar under the form of bread and wine; by your introduction of Roman Catholic books 'adapted to the use of our church'; by encouraging the use of rosaries and crucifixes and special devotions to our Lord, . . . you have done much to revive among us the system which may be pre-eminently called 'Sacramental'. And yet now, when, by God's mercy to us, a great opportunity has occurred of asserting and enforcing the very keystone of this system, . . . you seem to shrink from the front rank.

W. Dodsworth, *A Letter to the Revd E. B. Pusey* (1850), 16–17.

Though the hoped-for stream of converts did not come from the Church of England, another stream did add greatly to the numbers of the Roman Church in England. This was the stream of Irish immigrants brought over by the combined effect of poverty in Ireland and the needs of England for cheap labour. During the decade of the Great Famine of 1847, Irish immigration reached its peak, and the numbers of persons who were Irish born or of Irish descent settled in England could be numbered by tens of thousands. The great majority were Roman Catholics and among the poorest of paid labourers in London and the industrial towns. They swamped the old minority of native Roman Catholics, who were mostly upper class and well educated, and their advent accentuated the twofold nature of Roman Catholicism as expressed by a one-time member of that Church:

> Roman Catholicism is a dual system. There is first of all the popular religion—the cultus of the Sacred Heart, the Virgin, and the Saints, of votive candles and the hearing of Mass on Sundays. Secondly, there is what may be called esoteric Catholicism, the philosophy of the priests—and of rare philosophically-minded laymen. It is an amalgam of Christianity and Neoplatonism,* moulded and perfected during many centuries. Master craftsmen have worked on it—Augustine, Aquinas, Suarez. It is a coherent logical system of thought, glittering and shapely as a machine, . . . and few of the laity understand it. Their Catholicism is the religion of the candles burning before the statues, the incomprehensible but mystic Mass, and (in northern countries) a sternly Puritan way of life.

W. P. Witcutt, *Return to Reality* (1954), 18–22.

The thousands of Irish settlers inspired the growth of the popular form of Roman Catholicism, which was mistrusted and disliked by the old English priests and lay people, but welcomed by the new converts who wished Romanism to be as unlike Protestantism as possible. They were supported by Dr Nicholas Wiseman (1802–65), the son of Anglo-Irish parents and Rector of the English College at Rome from 1828 to 1840, when he returned to England to become one of the Vicars Apostolic, the title given to the eight Roman Catholic bishops in England who each administered a district of the country. He wanted the creation of Roman Catholic dioceses in England which would give his Church an organized, permanent position in the country; and he saw himself the head of the new hierarchy. He and his supporters brought pressure upon the Papacy to take this step. The influx of the Irish into England was represented as making it necessary for reasons of organization, while the Gorham case suggested that it would hasten still more the flood of converts expected from the Church of England. In August 1850 Wiseman was summoned to Rome, and early in October he issued a typically exuberant, florid pastoral letter 'from out of the Flaminian Gate' (i.e. the Porta del Popolo, the northern gate of the city of Rome, since etiquette forbade him to issue it within the papal walls):

> For on the twenty-ninth day of last month on the Feast of the Archangel Saint Michael, prince of the heavenly host, his Holiness Pope Pius IX was graciously pleased to issue his Letters Apostolic, under the Fisherman's Ring, conceived in terms of great weight and dignity, wherein he substituted for the eight Apostolic Vicariates heretofore existing, one archiepiscopal or metropolitan and twelve episcopal sees; repealing at the same time, and annulling all dispositions and enactments made for England by the Holy See with reference to its late form of ecclesiastical government.
>
> And by a brief dated the same day his Holiness was further pleased to appoint us, though most unworthy, to the archiepiscopal see of Westminster, established by the above-mentioned Letters Apostolic, giving us at the same time the administration of the episcopal see of Southwark. So that at present, and until such time as the Holy See should think fit otherwise, we govern, and shall continue to govern, the counties of Middlesex, Hertford, and Essex as ordinary thereof, and those of Surrey, Sussex, Kent, Berkshire and Hampshire, with the islands annexed, as administrator with ordinary jurisdiction.
>
> Further, we have to announce to you, dearly beloved in Christ, that, as if still further to add solemnity and honour before the Church to this noble act of Apostolic authority, and to give an additional mark of paternal benevolence towards us the Catholics of England, his Holiness was pleased to raise us, in the private consistory of Monday, the 30th of September, to the rank of Cardinal Priest of the holy Roman Church. And on the Thursday next ensuing, being the third day of this month of October, in public consistory, he delivered to us the insignia of this dignity, the cardinalitial hat; assigning us afterwards for our title in the private consistory which we attended, the Church of St Pudentiana, in which St Peter is groundedly believed to have enjoyed the hospitality of the noble

and partly British family of the Senator Pudens.

In that same consistory we were enabled ourselves to ask for the archiepiscopal Pallium for our new see of Westminster; and this day we have been invested, by the hands of the Supreme Pastor and Pontiff himself, with this badge of metropolitan jurisdiction.

Bernard Ward, *The Sequel to Catholic Emancipation* (2 vols, 1915), II, Appendix M.

Wiseman so little thought that this pastoral letter would cause any trouble that he ordered it to be read from the pulpits of all the churches in his new diocese on the next possible Sunday; but this action was only equalled by the imprudence of his words. The country was astonished. His emotional and rhetorical language seemed offensive and suggestive of exultation and pride. His claim to govern parts of England was provocative. There were indignant meetings held all over the country, and rioting broke out in some towns. The press was bitterly hostile and insisted that the royal prerogative had been invaded. Queen Victoria, however, was not herself alarmed. She did not believe that Roman Catholicism would ever make much headway in her kingdom. She did not fear it nearly as much as she did the Puseyites, whom she thought might destroy the Church of England. To the Duchess of Norfolk, who wrote to her deploring the encouragement the Pope's action had given to the proselytizing efforts of certain Roman Catholic priests, she replied:

I fully understand your anxiety relative to the proceedings of the Roman Catholic clergy, but I trust that there is no real danger to be apprehended from that quarter, the more so as I believe they see that they have been misled and misinformed as to the feeling of this country by some of the new converts to their religion. The real danger to be apprehended, and what I am certain has led to these proceedings on the part of the Pope, lies in *our own* divisions, and in the extraordinary conduct of the Puseyites. I trust that the eyes of many may now be opened. One would, however, much regret to see any acts of intolerance towards the many innocent people who I believe entirely disapprove of the injudicious conduct of their Church.

A. C. Benson & Viscount Esher (eds), *The Letters of Queen Victoria* (3 vols, 1908), II, 277.

Unfortunately, the Prime Minister, Lord John Russell, did not emulate the Queen's restraint. When his old friend, Dr Edward Maltby, Bishop of Durham, wrote to him publicly complaining about the 'insolent and insidious' nature of the 'Papal aggression' implied by the creation of the Roman Catholic hierarchy, Russell wrote a reply which Maltby published with his permission. In it Russell not only associated the government with the popular outcry against the Roman Catholics, but also identified the Puseyite party within the Church of England with the subversive designs of the Papacy:

> There is an assumption of power in all the documents which have come from Rome; a pretension of supremacy over the realm of England, and a claim to sole and undivided sway, which is inconsistent with the Queen's supremacy, with the rights of our bishops and clergy, and with the spiritual independence of the nation, as asserted even in Roman Catholic times.
>
> I confess, however, that my alarm is not equal to my indignation.
>
> Even if it shall appear that the ministers and servants of the Pope in this country have not transgressed the law, I feel persuaded that we are strong enough to repel any outward attacks. The liberty of Protestantism has been enjoyed too long in England to allow of any successful attempt to impose a foreign yoke upon our minds and consciences. No foreign prince or potentate will be at liberty to fasten his fetters upon a nation which has so long and so nobly vindicated its right to freedom of opinion, civil, political, and religious.
>
> Upon this subject, then, I will only say that the present state of the law shall be carefully examined, and the propriety of adopting any proceedings with reference to the recent assumption of power, deliberately considered.
>
> There is a danger, however, which alarms me much more than any aggression of a foreign sovereign.
>
> Clergymen of our own Church, who have subscribed the Thirty-Nine Articles and acknowledged in explicit terms the Queen's supremacy, have been most forward in leading their flocks 'step by step to the very verge of the precipice'. The honour paid to saints, the claim of infallibility for the Church, the superstitious use of the sign of the cross, the muttering of the liturgy so as to disguise the language in which it is written, the recommendation of auricular confession, and the administration of penance and absolution, all these things are pointed out by clergymen of the Church of England as worthy of adoption, and are now openly reprehended by the Bishop of London in his charge to the clergy of his diocese.
>
> What then is the danger to be apprehended from a foreign prince of no great power compared to the danger within the gates from the unworthy sons of the Church of England herself?

E. R. Norman, *op cit*, 159–61.

Though Russell had condemned the Puseyites at least as forcefully as the Roman Catholics, he had committed himself to legislation against the new Roman Catholic hierarchy. This eventually took the form of the Ecclesiastical Titles Act of 1851, which declared the Roman Catholic sees illegal. It was a retrograde piece of discriminatory legislation, demanded by the passing excitement of the time, but really contrary to the spirit of the age. As most people had foreseen, it was an empty law. No one was ever prosecuted under it, and it was repealed under Gladstone twenty years later:

> If after the passing of this Act, any Person shall obtain or cause to be procured from the Bishop or See of *Rome*, or shall publish or put in use within any Part of the United Kingdom, any such Bull, Brief, Rescript, or Letters Apostolic, or any other Instrument or Writing, for the Purpose of constituting such Archbishops or Bishops of such pretended Provinces, Sees, or Dioceses, within the United Kingdom, or of any Person, other than a Person thereunto authorized by Law in respect of an Archbishopric, Bishopric, or Deanery of the United Church of *England* and *Ireland*, assume or use the Name, Style, or Title of Archbishop, Bishop or Dean of any City, Town or Place, or of any Territory or District (under any Designation or Description whatsoever) in the United Kingdom, whether such City, Town or Place, or such Territory or District, be or be not the See or the Province, or co-extensive with the Province, of any Archbishop, or the See or the Diocese, or co-extensive with the Diocese, of any Bishop, or the Seat or Place of the Church of any Dean, or co-extensive with any Deanery, of the said United Church, the Person so offending shall for every such Offence forfeit and pay the Sum of One hundred Pounds, to be recovered as Penalties imposed by the recited Act may be recovered under the Provisions thereof, or by Action of Debt at the Suit of any Person in One of Her Majesty's Superior Courts of Law, with the Consent of Her Majesty's Attorney General in *England* and *Ireland*, or Her Majesty's Advocate in Scotland, as the Case may be.
> *English Historical Documents* (1957), vol XII (1), 370.

Meanwhile, the Roman Church had gained a convert who was to exercise the most powerful influence of any individual upon its place in English life. He was Henry Edward Manning (1808–92), who had been Archdeacon of Chichester since 1841. The archdeacons of the Church of England took an important part in implementing the administrative reforms initiated by the Ecclesiastical Commission, but Manning opposed this body from the start because he disliked the co-operation with the State which it implied. From being an Evangelical, he swung over to Tractarianism and (though knowing nothing about the Middle Ages) readily accepted the movement's backward look to a supposed time when the Church had been entirely free from control by princes and politicians. In 1848 he paid a visit to Rome and was received in private audience by Pope Pius IX, who raised his eyes to heaven and said, 'My poor prayers are offered every day for England'. The Eternal City at that time was still under papal rule, and the Archdeacon of Chichester returned home very much impressed. He wrote in his private diary:

> Strange thoughts have visited me. I have felt that the episcopate of the English Church is secularized and bound down beyond hope . . . Something keeps rising and saying, 'You will end in the Roman Church'.
>
> E. S. Purcell, *Life of Cardinal Manning* (2 vols, 1896), I, 49.

Such was his frame of mind, that the Gorham case was sufficient to push him into the Roman Church. The promulgation of the decision of the Judicial Committee of the Privy Council in 1850 (although it included as assessors the Archbishops of Canterbury and York, who both concurred in the decision) was to him a blatant example of dictation by the State to the Church. He published an open letter to the Bishop of Chichester on 'The Appellate Jurisdiction of the Crown in Matters Spiritual', and sought to organize a monster petition of the clergy against the Royal Supremacy; 'but only about 1,800 clergymen signed it out of 20,000, and I saw the game was up'. Masterful by nature, he never liked to find himself upon the losing side. As Sir Shane Leslie icily said, 'All that Manning conceived personally for the good of the Church was attributed to the inspiration of the Holy Ghost.' In 1851 he was received into the Roman Church. His archidiaconal colleague in Sussex, Julius Charles Hare (1795–1855), Archdeacon of Lewes, commented to his clergy on the secession:

> I can only wonder at the inscrutable dispensation by which such a man has been allowed to fall under so withering, soul-deadening a spell,—and repeat with awe, to myself and to my friends, 'Let him who thinketh he standeth take heed lest he fall'.
>
> Augustus J. C. Hare, *Memorials of a Quiet Life* (2 vols, 1874), II, 332–3.

Manning himself said on his secession, 'Now my career is ended'; but that was not to be so. Nineteen years later, as Archbishop of Westminster, he helped to force the doctrine of Papal Infallibility through the Vatican Council, and in 1875 he was made a Cardinal. Alone among all the Roman Catholic bishops in England during this period, he was equal in calibre to the Anglican bishops. Alone among them also, he made a valuable and important contribution to English public life.

> Of his appearance on the platform at Exeter Hall, at the meeting of the Agricultural Labourers' Union in December 1871, when he was the only ecclesiastic present, it may be said that it was in itself a courageous act and one that has opened a new era for all the churches. Since that day, the sight of clergymen, especially Nonconformists, taking part in such meetings has become familiar enough; and Manning himself eclipsed the memory of his earlier public effort on behalf of labour by the success of his similar undertakings in later years and especially in 1889. But the first bold step must not be forgotten.
>
> W. H. Hutton, *Life of H. E. Manning* (1892), 157.

With the exception of another Archdeacon, Robert Wilberforce (a brother of Bishop Wilberforce and friend of Manning), who went over in 1854, Manning was the last outstanding Anglican who became a Roman Catholic during this period. Henceforward, the Roman Church continued to grow in numbers and strength, but remained largely apart from the general life of the nation.

8 The Nonconformists

During the nineteenth century the Methodists continued to be the largest body among the Nonconformists in England, probably as numerous as the other bodies put together. They undoubtedly owed much of their success to the organization bequeathed by John Wesley. As an evangelist Wesley had set out to convince people through his preaching that they could only be saved by faith in an all-loving God, but it was as an administrator that he had kept his converts faithful to his teaching. Enrolled into local societies, they were further divided into classes under class-leaders, who visited them regularly in their homes and investigated their faith and morals. The weekly class-meetings for 'fellowship in Christian experience' were the basis of Methodist discipline and unity. There the members met regularly for hymns and prayers, to be exhorted and to share their experience with each other. A glimpse into the working of a class-meeting in about 1820 is given by this account, even though it is far from sympathetic:

> The class-meetings are held weekly. The classes ought, according to rule, to consist of ten or twelve members; but they sometimes contain as many as thirty, forty or fifty and at other times not more than three or four. Each member kneels down as soon as he enters, to pray a little by himself. The leader then begins the meeting by giving out a hymn, and the members stand up to sing. Then the leader prays, gives out another hymn and then tells his experience. Sometimes he tells what trials he has met with, and what deliverances he has experienced through the week, what joys and sorrows he has had, how he felt at the love-feast, the prayer-meeting or the fellowship-meeting, what liberty he had in secret prayer, how he felt by reading the Scriptures or hearing sermons or while busy at his work, what passages have come to his mind or what promises have been applied to his soul. At other times he simply tells how he feels at the moment; while at other times he says nothing about his experience or feelings, but just gives thanks to God for what He has done for him, in a general way, or offers a few words of exhortation or preaching to the members. He then asks each member in turn the

> state of his mind. A very common form of question is, 'Well, brother, or well, sister, how do you feel the state of your mind to-night?' At other times it will be, 'Well, brother, will you tell us what the Lord is doing for you?' Different leaders have different ways of proposing the question, and the same leader varies it at times. When the question is put, the member answers. Some of the members tell a long and flaming story; others say little or next to nothing. Some speak loud and even shout; others speak so low that they cannot be heard, either by the leaders or by the rest of the members. Some are always happy, according to their story; others are always doubtful and fearful and can never say much either about their feelings or performances. One tells you he has been on the sunny side all the week; another says he has been on the mount of transfiguration and that he could say with one of old, 'Master, it is good to be here'. Another has been with Moses on the top of Pisgah and got a view of the promised land. Another felt he was like the beloved disciple in the Isle of Patmos, in the spirit on the Lord's Day, and that he had not lost the blessing he received under the Sunday morning's sermon all the week through. It frequently happens that when the first has told a good experience, the rest follow the example; while when the first tells of troubles and trials, the rest generally speak of having had the same kind of trials or something similar. If the first is on a high key, they are almost all on a high key; but if the first be on a low key, the rest are on a low key too. There will generally be one or two in a large meeting that will tell a fine bright tale, let the rest tell what kind of tale they please; and there will generally be one or two in a large meeting that will tell a low, desponding story, let the rest tell what they will. Still, it commonly happens that the first person who speaks gives the turn to the meeting generally.
>
> J. T. Barker (ed), *The Life of Joseph Barker Written by Himself* (1880), 118.

The class-meetings with which this writer was familiar were those of the original or Wesleyan Methodists, who shared much of the founder's conservatism and respect for the Church of England. Many of their chapels used the Book of Common Prayer with slight alterations, and as late as 1870 a few refrained from celebrating the sacrament or from holding services during the hours of worship in the local parish church. Indeed, the connection with the Church, which Wesley had wished his followers to retain, was slow in breaking, and, in the end, it was probably the rise of Anglo-Catholicism that did much to kill it. Writing of his boyhood days in the 1860s in the small village of Crayke in Yorkshire, Dr W. R. Inge recalled:

> The high Churchmanship of those days would hardly be recognised as such now. Ecclesiastical millinery was totally neglected; I do not think that my grandfather ever wore a cassock. On the other hand, there was no hesitation in calling dissenters heretics, or schismatics, or both. The Church of England was the only religious body that had a right to exist. There was a small Wesleyan chapel in the village; but half the Methodists came to church once on Sundays, and all, I think, were married and buried by the rector. The stiffer Churchmanship of the next generation drove all such pious waverers into unmitigated Nonconformity.
>
> W. R. Inge, *Assessments and Anticipations* (1929), 15.

Such conservatism, however, did not satisfy all Methodists, especially those later converts who came from Nonconformist families and had a very different attitude towards the Church of England. Moreover, as Methodism became a settled religion, and its original members prospered, there were signs that it was ceasing to be a working-class faith, that Methodists were thinking of themselves as 'respectable' in comparison with the 'common people'. There were even complaints that in Methodist chapels this outlook was finding expression in the distinction between private pews and free seats. A leading Wesleyan minister wrote in the *Watchman* in 1849:

> Our chapels have been fitted up too much as private dwellings than as places of public worship; and the free sittings, if sufficient, not made readily perceivable nor easily accessible. I could name chapels with expensive architectural frontispieces of stone and with interior ornaments of 'dead white and gold' where the poor's seats are like sheep-pens, in the four corners of the building and behind the pulpit; and where, even then, the seats adjoining are screened off most carefully by high rods and curtains. I am no believer in the doctrine of 'equality' as it is now expounded by many—I regard it as foolish and contrary to the order of God ... But admitting all this, it is not only unbecoming but detrimental to Methodism (and it would be so to any church) thus to appear to neglect the poor.
>
> J. L. & Barbara Hammond, *The Bleak Age* (revised ed, 1947), 136.

A number of Methodists compared such chapels unfavourably with the early field preaching and simple meeting-houses of the early days under Wesley and his friends. As a result, there took place several secessions from the Methodist Conference by those who wished to engage in the more active ways of evangelism rather than to concentrate upon the pastoral care of congregations which was becoming the main work of many ministers and lay preachers of the later generation. The most active of these secessionist bodies were the Primitive Methodists who came into being in 1811. Their period of outstanding success was in the 1820s, and one of their preachers was Thomas Russell (1806–89), whose account of a day's preaching in 1830 is very reminiscent of the earlier experiences of Wesley himself:

> Sunday, April 4.—I preached in the open air at Ramsbury again, at seven in the morning, to several hundreds. About twenty young men sung wicked songs all the time, and shouted out, 'Church and King! No Ranters here! No preaching here.' Nevertheless the word preached had its desired effect; good was done. I went a third time. Numbers crowded round me as soon as I entered the place, children and young men ringing hand bells, sheep bells, horse bells, and blowing horns, and shouting at a strange pitch. I walked through the place amidst hundreds of spectators. Towards the lower part of the town a Baptist minister's widow, with true sympathy and kindness, and with heroic courage, rushing into the midst of these ruffians, cried shame upon them for their conduct and took me into her house. She gave me some refreshment and spoke kindly to me, saying, 'You are like Paul and Silas at Philippi, but the Lord will stand by you.' After resting a few minutes and praying with this kind friend, I again encountered the mob, and crossing to a heap of stones I ascended it and preached as well as I could collect my thoughts. At the close I told them if they would behave better I would send them a female to preach, and then left them. About twenty youths, influenced by a better spirit, followed me nearly a mile out of the town, and on bidding them farewell I told them I would pray with them. We all kneeled down and while at prayer most of them wept. There was evidently a good work begun in their youthful minds. This very much encouraged me, and though sorrowful I could rejoice.

Thomas Russell, *Autobiography* (1889), 27–8.

Such evangelism increased Nonconformity's numbers among the working-classes, and its growing strength encouraged its members to redouble their efforts to obtain civil equality. The Test and Corporation Acts were the first object of their attack. An Annual Act of Indemnity had long absolved persons who ignored the requirement that they should receive the Holy Communion as a condition of holding any kind of national or local office; but Nonconformists resented the inequality implied in these measures. An important move in their campaign against the Acts was the formation of the Protestant Society for the Protection of Religious Liberty in 1811, an organization which for the first time was on a national basis and united the Methodists with the older Nonconformist bodies. In January 1828 a resolution of the Society asserted:

That the Committee have been delighted by the wide spreading and noble enthusiasm with which their letters were greeted, and by the numerous and respectable petitions transmitted to other public bodies, as well as to them, and by which the House of Commons were greatly impressed: yet they would anxiously urge all congregations and other friends to the repeal of these acts, by whom these petitions were sent, to apply to their own County and Borough members to grant the measure the succour of their influence as well as their vote.

Norman Gash (ed), *The Age of Peel* (1968), 19.

By then success was at hand for them. The repeal of the Acts that year was due partly to the support they received from many churchmen who, despite doubts about the equal relief it would bring Roman Catholics, recognized the immorality of using religious observances for political purposes. An article in the Evangelical periodical, the *Christian Observer*, for March 1828 stated:

The penal effects of these acts have long been set aside by the annual indemnity bill; but the acts themselves remained unrepealed, vexatious though impotent, irritating the Dissenter without benefiting the Church; and, worse than this, a parochial clergyman is legally bound, under an exposure to heavy damages, to administer the sacred ordinance of the Lord's Supper to the most profligate man in his parish, who may choose to demand it at his hands, as 'a pick-lock to a palace'. Multitudes of religious persons, who differ widely as to their views on the general question whether a test is necessary or likely to be efficient, perfectly concur in opinion as to the gross impropriety of the particular test in question.

Ibid, 19.

Having secured this triumph, the Nonconformists went on to demand the removal of the rest of their grievances. They were permitted to conduct their own marriage ceremonies in 1836, but perhaps the most keenly felt of their grievances were Church Rates, which vestries had long been empowered to levy for the upkeep of the parish church and churchyard. A growing number of Nonconformists refused to pay them and had their possessions seized or were imprisoned. The leader of the campaign was John Bright (1811–89), the orator and statesman, who was a Quaker. Speaking in Parliament in 1839, he appealed to churchpeople to support the abolition of Church Rates as they had the repeal of the Test* and Corporation* Acts:

Am I appealing in vain to you, when I try to encourage you to believe that if there were no Church rates the members of your Church and of your congregation would be greatly multiplied, and that, as has taken place in the parish where I live, your Churches would be better supported by your own voluntary and liberal contributions than they can ever be by the penny per pound issuing from the pockets of men who do not attend your Church, and who are rendered ten times more hostile to it by the very effort to make them contribute to its support.

C. Sylvester Horne, *Nonconformity in the Nineteenth Century* (1912), 59.

The Church Rates were eventually abrogated by Act of Parliament in 1868; and in 1871 all religious tests were abolished at the universities. By then, however, many Nonconformists, instead of demanding relief from particular grievances, had moved on to campaign for the disestablishment and disendowment of the Church of England. The tone of the movement may be gathered from an extract from a letter written by George Hadfield, the Congregationalist author and politician, in the *Baptist Magazine* for December 1833:

> We are required to submit to the domination of a corrupt state church; to be governed by bishops; to see £3,500,000 at the least (but more likely £5,000,000) annually expended in the maintenance of a clergy, of whom a vast majority do not preach the gospel; to see the cure of souls bought and sold in open market; to have the Universities closed against us, and all the iniquities of those degraded places continued; to be taxed, tithed and rated to the support of a system which we abjure; to be compelled to submit to objectionable rites and ceremonies at marriage, baptism and burial;—in one word, to be left out of the social compact and degraded . . . We have hitherto demanded too little; and, consequently, we have been refused everything worth caring about. The bill for relieving places of worship from the poor-rates, which was the fruit of the labours of the last session of Parliament, is no boon to us. It applies to churches in the establishment more than to ourselves, and I doubt whether it will save the Dissenters £50 a year. I fear we have even misled the government itself by asking for trifles, when we ought to have been contending for great principles. What signifies a small church-rate, when we ought to be contending against a corrupt state church? What is the trifling amount of poor rates levied upon a very few of our chapels, in comparison of millions of pounds annually expended on a secular and dominant clergy?—and all this done in a country burdened with a debt which grinds us all!

Norman Gash, *op cit*, 54.

Though by the later part of the nineteenth century, many of Nonconformity's grievances had been remedied, the campaign for disestablishment continued throughout this period. The Church of Ireland was disestablished in 1869, and the Church in Wales was on the brink of disestablishment by the end of this period; but the great prize desired by the Nonconformists, the disestablishment of the Church of England, eluded their grasp, though it was the one topic of public interest on which, according to Matthew Arnold in his *Culture and Anarchy* (1869), organizers could 'be certain of having a crowded meeting in any large town in England' in almost any decade of the nineteenth century. From the start the principle of establishment was not without supporters. One of these was Samuel Taylor Coleridge (1772–1834), who stated in his *Concluding Address to the Parliamentary Leaders of the Liberalists and Utilitarians*:

> I respect the talents of many, and the motives and character of some, among you too sincerely to court the scorn which I anticipate. But neither shall the fear of it prevent me from declaring aloud, and as a truth which I hold it the disgrace and calamity of a professed statesman not to know and acknowledge, that a permanent, nationalized, learned order, a national clerisy or Church is an essential element of a rightly constituted nation, without which it wants the best security alike for its permanence and its progression; and for which neither tract societies nor conventicles, nor Lancastrian schools, nor mechanics' institutions, nor lecture bazaars under the absurd name of universities, nor all these collectively, can be a substitute. For they are all marked with the same asterisk of spuriousness, shew the same distemper-spot on the front, that they are empirical specifics for morbid symptoms that help to feed and continue the disease.
>
> But you wish for general illumination: you would spur-arm the toes of society: you would enlighten the higher ranks *per ascensum ab imis*. You begin, therefore, with the attempt to popularize science: but you will only effect its plebification. It is folly to think of making all, or the many, philosophers, or even men of science and systematic knowledge. But it is duty and wisdom to aim at making as many as possible soberly and steadily religious; inasmuch as the morality which the State requires in its citizens for its own well-being and ideal immortality, and without reference to their spiritual interest as individuals, can only exist for the people in the form of religion. But the existence of a true philosophy, or the power and habit of contemplating particulars in the unity and fontal mirror of the idea, this in the rulers and teachers of a nation is indispensable to a sound state of religion in all classes. In fine, religion, true or false, is and ever has been the centre of gravity in a realm, to which all other things must and will accommodate themselves.

S. T. Coleridge, *On the Constitution of Church and State According to the Idea of Each* (1839), 28.

Such arguments were capable of influencing only a few people, and the reasons for the failure of the campaign for disestablishment have been variously explained: the fact that the Nonconformists were disunited, that the Methodists were conservative or that Gladstone was an Anglican; but probably the main reason was that the Nonconformists, although they perhaps formed about thirty per cent of the population in 1860 when at their height, failed to gain the support of the most influential part of public opinion. Many, like Matthew Arnold, disliked them because of their 'separation from the main current of national life', and their narrowness:

> To the many who think that spirituality and sweetness and light are all moonshine, this will not appear to matter much; but with us, who value them, and who think that we have traced much of our present discomfort to the want of them, it weighs a great deal. So not only do we say that the Nonconformists have got provincialism and lost totality by the want of a religious establishment, but we say that the very example which they bring forward to help their case makes against them; and when they triumphantly show us America without religious establishments, they only show us a whole nation touched, amidst its greatness and promise with that provincialism which it is our aim to extirpate in the English Nonconformists.
>
> Matthew Arnold, *Culture and Anarchy* (1869), xif.

Towards the end of the century there was, indeed, a general feeling that Nonconformity suffered from 'failing vitality' and was in decline. Nonconformists themselves had to admit that they were unable to meet the problems of the time as actively as the Church of England. Earlier in the century they had built large chapels in the centres of towns, which had been well-attended, but by now many people were moving out into the suburbs. The old central places of worship were deserted, but they were not being adequately replaced in the new suburban areas. An early report of the church extension committee of the Congregational Union of England and Wales gave these results of an inquiry among local congregations:

> To the question, 'In your judgment are the churches in your district able, separately or collectively, to undertake further Church Extension?' only twelve positively answered 'Yes'; three answered, 'if needed'; one replied 'if united'; one 'not now'; while forty-two blankly answer, 'No'. And this negative answer comes from districts, many of them, where vigorous action is most urgently called for.
>
> *Congregational Year Book* (1894), 69.

One of the main reasons why Nonconformity did not increase during the later part of the nineteenth century was the considerable defection of its members to the Church of England. This took place on the part of ministers as well as laymen. The superior social position of the Anglican clergymen (though his financial position might be inferior) inevitably attracted some Nonconformist ministers, but others were influenced by the wider sphere of labour open to the clergy in their parishes. The minister often worked only in a small circle of tradesmen or respectable artisans who were members of his sect, while the clergyman was widely accepted and often had more opportunities to minister to the poor. Not infrequently a Nonconformist minister was prepared to make the change even though it involved financial sacrifice. When the father of Eric Gill, the sculptor, who was Assistant Minister at the Countess of Huntingdon's Church in Brighton, joined the Church of England in 1897, he was accused of making 'a move in the direction of better income and better status', but his son said that he reduced his income by £150 a year when he was accepted by the Bishop of Chichester, for:

> The grand economic result was a curacy at Chichester with £90 a year, followed by one at Bognor with very little more (I don't know the figure) and then no preferment at all until, in 1913, at the age of sixty-four, he was presented to the obscure vicarage of West Wittering, near Chichester, with an annual income of little over two hundred pounds. And that was the grand climax in the career of a man who was said to have joined the Church of England for the sake of money and high society.
>
> Eric Gill, *Autobiography* (1940), 66.

Nonconformist ministers were prepared to accept lower stipends by making such moves because to an increasing number of them, the negative, protesting, sectional outlook of their bodies made no appeal. The idea of a Church with a national mission to society as a whole seemed much more worthwhile. They were attracted by the new spirit in the Church, especially in the form in which it was presented by such a moderate, comprehending, efficient churchman as Mandell Creighton, who became Bishop of London in 1897:

> He took his stand for God, and made his great decision at the extreme hour of intellectual tension, when the panic roused by the new criticism was at its height, and when the victorious efficacy of the scientific and critical methods appeared to have swept the field. It is difficult for us now to gauge the dismay of that bad

> hour. At the close of the sixties it seemed to us at Oxford almost incredible that a young don of any intellectual reputation for modernity should be on the Christian side. And Creighton by temperament lay open to the full force of the prevailing movement. No one could be more acutely sensitive to all that the critical spirit had to say. No one lent himself more freely to the aesthetic and other non-Christian influences of that distracted time. Yet, in spite of the swirling flood in which he found himself plunged, his inner steadiness of thought and will kept the balance.
>
> Memorial Sermon Preached in St Paul's Cathedral, 1901, quoted, Louise Creighton, *Life and Letters of Mandell Creighton* (2 vols, 1904), I, 75.

What should Nonconformity do in such a situation? How were the sects to go beyond 'our quiet, respectable world of prayerful shopkeepers' (as Eric Gill called it) and evangelize the masses? William Booth (1829–1912), who had become dissatisfied as a lay-preacher with the existing congregations of respectable Methodists, had his own answer to the question. In 1865 he formed the Salvation Army, which sought to evanglize the poor (as Mrs Booth put it) 'by people of their own ideas, who would speak to them in a language they understood and reach them by means suited to their own tastes'. The devotion and courage of the Salvationists impressed many people, who expected great things of their efforts:

> The fortresses of Beelzebub are music-halls, penny gaffs, dancing-rooms and the like; of these, in London and elsewhere, the Salvation Army has stormed no less than one hundred and has turned these haunts of ribaldry into places of divine service ... Most of our secular efforts to raise the masses have simply failed because of their inability to set the hearts of the populace aflame. The strength of Mr Booth seems to be that he unites two powers: he preaches doctrines that fill the face of a believer with light and radiance, and he is no less thorough in enforcing a complete reform of life.
>
> *The Saturday Review* (1879), quoted, E. K. Milliken, *The Victorian Era* (1963), 124.

The traditional Nonconformist bodies, however, did little to identify themselves with Booth's new strategy of salvation. Indeed, R. W. Dale (1829–95), the most honoured of Congregational ministers, went so far as to say that Congregationalists should not expect their denomination to engage in a mission to the poor:

> The vigorous and the cultivated need salvation as well as the ignorant and the wretched. The intellect as well as the heart has to be claimed for Christ, and it is the special duty of Congregationalists so to present the Christian gospel as to

> draw those who are never likely to be reached by the Salvation Army, and so to discipline them to the highest intellectual and ethical perfection.
>
> A. W. W. Dale, *The Life of R. W. Dale* (1898), 613.

There were those who violently disagreed with Dale, especially the younger generation of Nonconformists, who replied sharply to him in the *British Weekly* and asserted roundly, 'The Congregationalist ministers of the future are not called to any apostolate of prigdom'; but the attitude of Nonconformists as a whole showed that they fundamentally shared Dale's outlook. Moreover, after the first successes achieved by its shock tactics up and down the country, doubts set in about the mission of the Salvation Army. It seemed that it was not likely to achieve more than the older sects in bringing the gospel to the masses. A detached survey of the Army, written in 1891, gives this account as typical of the effect of the arrival of a contingent of Salvationists in any part of the country:

> Its arrival creates a great ferment; during the first few months it gains a band of adherents, and there are some wonderful instances, which cannot be gainsaid, of moral reform. But then the progress of the Army in this particular place comes to an end. Its services are still held; but adherents are now added one by one at long intervals, and the 'Corps' is as little likely to affect the regeneration of the 'residuum' in that district as any of the surrounding religious bodies. Hence the growth of the Army in numbers has not been a steady and sustained growth in their earlier fields of labour: it is the result of the constant establishment of fresh corps in new places.
>
> W. J. Ashley, 'General Booth's Panacea', *Political Science Quarterly*, VI (1891), 550.

9 The Broad Churchmen

On 19th February 1861, the Revd Benjamin John Armstrong, Vicar of East Dereham in Norfolk, wrote in his diary:

> Ruridecanal Chapter at Yaxham. About thirteen clergy present. The regular subject—viz, Sunday Schools—named by the Bishop, was soon disposed of, and we then proceeded to consider whether we ought not to protest against *Essays and Reviews*, the infidel and unsettling tendency of which is greatly to be deplored. The Bench of Bishops has unanimously condemned the book. But in our little Chapter a difficulty arose, inasmuch that no one present had seen the book except myself. Fortunately I had in my pocket a long list of quotations from it which was read to the meeting. A protest was signed unanimously.
>
> B. J. Armstrong, *A Norfolk Diary* (1949), 77–8.

The book which these rural clergymen condemned, had been published the previous year. It was a collection of essays by seven authors, who wrote quite independently of each other and were responsible for their respective essays only, but shared a common belief in the necessity of free inquiry in religious matters. One of the essayists, John Percival (1834–1918), then a Fellow of Queen's College, Oxford, and afterwards Bishop of Hereford, described the genesis of the volume:

> The book owes its origin to some conversation between Mr Jowett and myself, as far back as eight or nine years ago, on the great amount of reticence in every class of society in regard to religious views—the melancholy unwillingness of people to state honestly their opinions in points of doctrine. We thought it might encourage free and honest discussion of Biblical topics, if we were to combine with some others to publish a volume of essays . . . one stipulation being made, that nothing should be written which was inconsistent with the position of ministers of our Church.
>
> E. G. Sandford (ed), *Memoirs of Archbishop Temple* (2 vols, 1906), II, 225.

The most significant and perhaps the most debated essay in the book was that by

Benjamin Jowett (1817–93), then Regius Professor of Greek at Oxford and afterwards Master of Balliol College. This is his own summary of its contents:

> Of what has been said, this is the sum:—That Scripture, like other books, has one meaning, which is to be gathered from itself without reference to the adaptations of Fathers or Divines; and without regard to *a priori* notions about its nature and origin. It is to be interpreted like other books, with attention to the character of its authors, and the prevailing state of civilization and knowledge, with allowance for peculiarities of style and language, and modes of thought and figures of speech. Yet not without a sense that as we read there grows upon us the witness of God in the world, anticipating in a rude and primitive age the truth that was to be, shining more and more unto the perfect day in the life of Christ, which again is reflected from different points of view in the teaching of His Apostles.

Benjamin Jowett, 'On the Interpretation of Scripture', *Essays and Reviews* (12th ed, 1869), 490–1.

Another essay, 'The National Church', was written by Henry Bristow Wilson (1803–88), Fellow of St John's College, Oxford, who had been one of four Oxford tutors to protest against Tract 90, but had since changed his ideas. Then he had asserted that the Tract went beyond the permitted 'liberty of interpreting the formularies of our Church', but now he insisted that the Church of England as a National Church must allow the greatest freedom of doctrinal belief to its members. A passage which caused much offence was one denying the doctrine that wicked men are irretrievably damned and will be punished for ever in the next life:

> The Christian Church can only tend those who are committed to its care, to the verge of that abyss which parts this world from the world unseen. Some of them fostered by her are now ripe for entering on a higher career: the many are but rudimentary spirits—germinal souls? What shall become of them? If we look abroad in the world and regard the neutral character of the multitude, we are at loss to apply to them, either the promises, or the denunciations of revelation . . . The Roman Church has imagined a *limbus infantium*. We must rather entertain a hope that there shall be found, after the great adjudication, receptacles suitable for those who shall be infants, not as to years of terrestrial, but as to spiritual development—nurseries as it were and seed-grounds, where the undeveloped may grow up under new conditions—the stunted may become strong, and the perverted be restored.

Henry Bristow Wilson, '*Séances Historiques de Genève*—The National Church', *Essays and Reviews*, 247–8.

The essay by Baden-Powell (1796–1860), Savilian Professor of Geometry at Oxford, was also provoking, though his thoughts were somewhat concealed by his involved style. He was a remarkable man, a radical theologican and possessed of an outstanding, assured intellect. He had three wives in succession and thirteen children, the twelfth of whom founded the Boy Scouts. As a clerical scientist, he annoyed both Evangelicals and Tractarians by condemning Scriptural and ecclesiastical miracles alike:

> To conclude, an alleged miracle can only be regarded in one of two ways;—either (1) abstractedly as a physical event, and therefore to be investigated by reason and physical evidence, and referred to physical causes, possibly to *known* causes, but at all events to some higher cause or law, if at present unknown; it then ceases to be supernatural, yet still might be appealed to in support of religious truth, especially as referring to the state of knowledge and apprehension of the parties addressed in past ages; or (2) as connected with religious doctrine, regarded in a sacred light, asserted on the authority of inspiration. In this case it ceases to be capable of investigation by reason, or to own its dominion; it is accepted on religious grounds, and can appeal only to the principle and influence of faith.

Baden-Powell, 'On the Study of the Evidences of Christianity', *Essays and Reviews*, 170.

When it first appeared, the volume attracted little attention, but at the beginning of 1861 Bishop Wilberforce denounced it in an elaborate and strongly worded article in the *Quarterly Review*, which aroused general interest and led to a flood of addresses, memorials and remonstrances to the archbishops and bishops. None of the ideas put forward by the essayists was new. German theologians in particular had long been discussing them; but neither the Evangelical nor the Anglo-Catholic revival had made the Church of England receptive to them. The publication of Charles Darwin's *The Origin of Species* in 1859 increased the desire to close the ranks against all doubts. The general attack on the essayists was not because of what they said, but because they said it; as was shown when a meeting of the bishops in 1861 at Fulham, urged on by Wilberforce, put forward a condemnation of the book. This the Archbishop of Canterbury, J. B. Sumner, issued as a reply to one of the addresses:

> REVEREND SIR,—I have taken the opportunity of meeting many of my Episcopal brethren in London to lay your address before them.
>
> They unanimously agree with me in expressing the pain it has given them that

any clergyman of our Church should have published such opinions as those concerning which you have addressed us.

We cannot understand how these opinions can be held consistently with an honest subscription to the formularies of our Church, with many of the fundamental doctrines of which they appear to us essentially at variance.

Whether the language in which these views are expressed is such as to make the publication an act which could be visited in the Ecclesiastical Courts, or to justify the Synodical condemnation of the book which contains them, is still under our gravest consideration. But our main hope is our reliance on the blessing of God, in the continued and increasing earnestness with which we trust that we and the clergy of our several dioceses may be enabled to teach and preach that good deposit of sound doctrine which our Church teaches in its fulness, and which we pray that she may, by God's grace, ever set forth as the uncorrupted Gospel of our Lord Jesus Christ.

R. T. Davidson & W. Benham, *Life of A. C. Tait*, I, 282.

This condemnation brought forward protests from those who shared the outlook of the essayists. Prominent among these was Arthur Penrhyn Stanley (1815–81), then Professor of Ecclesiastical History at Oxford and soon to be Dean of Westminster, whose favourite text, 'I see that all things come to an end, but Thy commandment is exceeding broad' (Psalm 119), was probably responsible for the term 'Broad Churchmen', applied to those who shared his views. He thought that *Essays and Reviews* was inexpedient, but regarded the attack on the book as much worse than anything contained in the book itself, and here he had the support of Brooke Foss Westcott (1825–1901), later to be Bishop of Durham, who wrote to him:

I think that the Essayists committed something worse than an error in addressing such a series of essays *ad populum*, when the mass of intelligent readers are at present wholly unfit to form a calm judgment on questions involving many of the nicest points of criticism. But, on the other hand, it seems to me to be no less dangerous to appeal to tradition alone as an answer to speculations which rest on admitted discoveries later than the source of the tradition. No one can have followed the course of theological inquiry in Germany without foreseeing that we in England must pass through—not a similar, I trust, but—a corresponding ordeal. I am fully convinced that Holy Scripture has nothing to fear from the most searching criticism.

Arthur Westcott, *Brooke Foss Westcott* (1905), 135–6.

Such an attitude, however, was very uncommon. Little attempt was made to consider on an intellectual level the points made by the essayists. They were (all mostly) dismissed by their opponents as heretics who had no place within the Church of England. Mark Pattison later, though writing in a typically bitter way, spoke justly of the obsolete outlook among the clergy. He accused them of upholding a form of Christianity in which there seemed to be no place for anyone with a critical intelligence and informed knowledge about the latest developments in theological scholarship:

> So wholly extinct is scientific theology in the Church of England that the English public could not recognize such a thing as a neutral and philosophic enquiry into the causes of the form of thought existing at any period. Our clergy know only of pamphlets which must be for or against one of the parties in the Church . . . This attempt to present the English public with a philosophical monograph on one special phase of English thought was singularly unsuccessful. To judge from the reviews, it never occurred to any of our public instructors that such a conception was possible.
>
> Mark Pattison, *Memoirs*, 314.

Legal action was taken against two of the essayists, H. B. Wilson and R. Williams, who were condemned to deprivation* for a year, but they secured the reversal of this verdict by the Judicial Committee of the Privy Council. That Court consisted of the Lord Chancellor (Richard Bethell, first Baron Westbury) and three lay lords together with the two archbishops and Bishop Tait. It disclaimed any intention of defining anew the doctrine of the Church or even of pronouncing upon the orthodoxy of the book as a whole. Its members had before them solely certain extracts which had come up from the lower court, one of these being the passage (already quoted) from Wilson's essay. The concluding words of the judgment delivered by Westbury were marked by the power of sarcastic speech for which he was noted:

> We are not required or at liberty to express any opinion upon the mysterious question of the eternity of final punishment, further than to say that we do not find in the Formularies,* to which this article refers, any such distinct declaration of our Church upon the subject, as to require us to condemn as penal the expression of hope by a clergyman that even the ultimate pardon of the wicked, who are condemned in the day of judgment, may be consistent with the will of Almighty God.
>
> Quoted S. C. Carpenter, *Church and People*, 511.

The three lay lords and Tait concurred with this judgment, though the two archbishops dissented. This was an outcome which caused great alarm in the Church among both clergy and laity. Finally, the book was condemned by a large majority in both houses of the Convocation of Canterbury. The fundamental basis of the resentment aroused by *Essays and Reviews* was the fear that it was attacking the authority of the Bible. It was this fear which united Dr Pusey and Lord Shaftesbury in protesting against the book. Practically all churchpeople, whether belonging to the Evangelical or Anglo-Catholic movements or neither, upheld the inerrancy of the Bible and did not believe that the attitude of the essayists could be reconciled with the Christian religion. On the day after *Essays and Reviews* had been censured by Convocation, *The Times* summed up the situation:

> It is ... an awkward prospect which we have before us, if we are to look forward now to a struggle of a class of parochial clergy with the creed of their congregations. There are many minute distinctions of doctrine about which these congregations do not care, but there is one authority upon which they do stand, and that is the authority of Scripture. The Bible, with its facts and its doctrines, naturally interpreted, is undoubtedly the religion of Protestant England. Our clergy, then, have a considerable latitude allowed them, but any theory which brings them into collision with the Bible, depriving it of its character as a record of certain actual facts connected with the foundation of our faith, idealizing these facts, and, in short, making the Bible a totally different thing from what the common belief supposes it to be—such a theory does appear to unfit a clergyman for the practical duties of a parish priest; because he is, in fact, in diametrical opposition to his parishioners with respect to the very basis of Christianity and the very foundation of their faith. He is in a false relation to them, which, whether clearly known by them or not, is a fundamental defect in his position: and if he preaches openly what he thinks there is no parish in England in which he could stay a week.
>
> *The Times*, 1st July 1861.

The alarm caused by the publication of *Essays and Reviews* was increased by the writings of John William Colenso (1814–83), a poor Cornish boy who obtained a scholarship to Cambridge, where he studied mathematics, and who in 1853 was appointed the first Bishop of the newly constituted see of Natal in South Africa. There the difficulties and questions of his Zulu converts led him into the field of Biblical and doctrinal criticism. In 1861 he issued a *Commentary on the Epistle to the Romans*, which through its rejection of eternal punishment and denial of much sacramental teaching provoked indignant protests; and even more determined opposition was aroused by his papers on *The Pentateuch and the Book of Joshua Critically Examined*, which through its rejection of eternal punishment and denial of much sacramental ship and historical accuracy of the Old Testament books. An example of the attacks made upon him may be seen in these extracts from the Preface to a pamphlet issued in 1863 and entitled simply *Moses, or the Zulu?* The Preface was written by John Charles Ryle, a strong Evangelical who in 1880 was to be appointed the first Bishop of Liverpool:

> Bishop Colenso's famous book, in my humble judgement, is so exceedingly weak and open to criticism that I do not expect it will do much harm . . . I never could have believed it possible that a highly-educated Cambridge man, and a Clergyman, could have seen so many difficulties in the Pentateuch where none really exist, and where a closer and more accurate study of the Bible would have shown him that it is he, and not Moses, who has made mistakes . . . Again, I never could have believed it possible that any one calling himself a Christian would have so coolly ignored God's *miraculous agency* as the plain solution of some of his supposed difficulties. Had the book come from an anonymous author, I should have said, 'This man is an infidel. He evidently regards miracles as a kind of perilous lumber, which must be thrown overboard at any risk.' Yet the author is a professing Christian! . . . Finally, I never could have believed it possible that any Bishop of the Church of England could put forth such a book, and yet retain office for a single day as a minister of the Church of England, much less as a Bishop . . . If nothing is done by those who ought to move in the matter, and the Bishop of Natal is let alone, . . . the Church of England will be disgraced in the eyes of Christendom, as a Church whose Bishops went to the stake for truth in the sixteenth century, but tolerated undisguised infidelity within her pale in 1863 . . .

> MOSES, OR THE ZULU? *A Detailed Reply to the Objections contained in Parts I and II of Bishop Colenso's Work*. By the Revd W. Wickes, MA, formerly Scholar of Trinity College, Cambridge; Professor of Mathematics in the University of Montreal; and Rector of the High School, Quebec; and now Association Secretary of the Colonial and Continental Church Society. With a Preface by the Revd J. C. Ryle, BA, Vicar of Stradbroke, Suffolk. Rom iii. 4 (London: 1863).

Colenso's conclusions about Mosaic chronology and statistics are nowadays accepted as among the assured results of critical research, though he wrote as a mathematician, and his concentration upon such questions as the number of men, women and children that could be accommodated within the Jewish Temple did not take into account the spiritual value of the Old Testament. As F. D. Maurice wrote:

> His idea of history is that it is a branch of arithmetic . . . To have a quantity of criticism about the dung in the Jewish camp, and the division of a hare's foot, thrown in my face, when I was satisfied that the Jewish history had been the mightiest witness to the people for a living God against the dead dogmas of priests, was more shocking to me than I can describe.
>
> Quoted, A. O. J. Cockshut, *Anglican Attitudes* (1959), 94–5.

In 1863 Colenso was declared deposed by his Metropolitan, Robert Gray, Bishop of Cape Town, but he denied the Bishop of Cape Town's jurisdiction, and the dispute now became an ecclesiastical rather than a theological controversy. Most church-people, however, continued to see the issue in the terms originally conceived by Colenso. He had said of his examination of the Pentateuch, 'It is a simple question of *facts*,' and his opponents, though they did not accept his conclusions, took the same attitude. If the Bible were not accurate in every respect, then it could not be taken as the foundation of Christian belief. Uncertainty of belief, brought about by the discarding of traditional viewpoints through intellectual inquiry, led them to reject intellectual speculation and insist upon the authority of divine revelation. John Henry Newman was expressing a widespread attitude when he wrote in 1852:

> In a state of society such as ours, in which authority, prescription, tradition, habit, moral instinct, and the divine influences go for nothing, in which free discussion and fallible judgment are prized as the birthright of each individual, I must be excused if I exercise towards this age, as regards its belief in this doctrine, some portion of that scepticism which it exercises itself towards every received but unscrutinized assertion whatever.
>
> J. H. Newman, *Idea of a University* (1912), 37.

There were, indeed, a number of churchpeople who regretted that so much of the time and energy of the Church should be given over to vehement, though often unintelligent, theological controversy, which they feared was diverting its members, and particularly the clergy, from giving their attention to other and more practical matters. This view was expressed by Charles Kingsley (1819–75) with his native robustness and intellectual vagueness in a letter about *Essays and Reviews* to C. R. Sumner, Bishop of Winchester, in 1861:

> I confess to having thrust away the book in disgust, as saying once again, very weakly, what I had long put out of sight and mind, in the practical realities of parish work. When my new curate came back to me after ordination, having heard your lordship's allusion to the *Essays and Reviews*, and asked me whether he should read them, I told him, 'By no means. They will disturb your mind with questions which you are too young to solve. Stick to the old truths and the old paths, and learn their divineness by sick beds and in every-day work and do not darken your mind with intellectual puzzles, which may breed disbelief, but can never breed vital religion or practical usefulness.

Charles Kingsley, *Letters and Memories of his Life* (2 vols, 1883), II, 123.

The effect of a generally conservative outlook in theology was to brand the Broad Churchmen as dangerous underminers of the faith. Yet, though they were a small minority in the Church, their ideas did steadily, though gradually, spread, especially among the more learned clergy. Frederick William Farrar (1831–1903), the author of the tear-jerking schoolboy novel, *Eric, or Little by Little*, and also a considerable theologian, wrote towards the end of his life, when he was Dean of Canterbury, about his experiences in connection with the *Dictionary of the Bible*, edited by Sir William Smith and published between 1860 and 1863:

> I had been asked to write the article on 'Deluge' for Smith's Dictionary of the Bible. I wrote it, but took views about the non-*universality* of the Deluge which most inquirers now hold. The editor and publisher, alarmed at this deviation from stereotyped opinion, postponed the insertion of the article; and in vol I inserted 'Deluge: see Flood'. But even when they had got as far as 'Flood' they had not made up their minds, and said 'Flood: see Noah'. My article was subsequently sacrificed; for Noah had been assigned to the present Bishop of Worcester. Yet, after all, Dr Perowne (as he then was) came to much the same conclusion as myself; for he wrote, 'that even the language used with regard to the Flood itself—strong as it undoubtedly is—*does not oblige us to suppose that the Deluge was universal*'.

R. Farrar, *Life of Frederick William Farrar* (1904), 113.

Slow though the influence of the Broad Churchmen was, they had within ten years of the publication of *Essays and Reviews* probably made it impossible for a large number of churchpeople to hold wholly to the notion of the infallibility of Scripture or to consider that all parts of it were equally the Word of God. Stanley asserted:

Charles Kingsley

> There are not above fifty clergymen in England who fully and from their hearts believe the precepts of Leviticus or the pedigrees of the Book of Chronicles, the description of the hare as a ruminant animal or the imprecations of Nehemiah on his enemies to be immediately and absolutely the Word of God, in the same sense, or anything like the same sense, as they believe this of the Sermon on the Mount or the farewell discourses in St John's Gospel.
>
> A. P. Stanley, *Essays on Church and State* (1870), 123.

The most striking sign of the triumph of the ideas of the Broad Churchmen was provided by the appearance of another book of essays, *Lux Mundi*, in 1889. Its authors were not themselves Broad Churchmen, but Anglo-Catholics, the editor of the book being Charles Gore (1853–1932), who had been appointed the first Principal of Pusey House, the institution founded at Oxford in memory of the Tractarian leader. It was sub-titled 'A Series of Studies in the Religion of the Incarnation', and its Preface asserted that its purpose was 'to attempt to put the Catholic faith into its right relation to modern intellectual and moral problems'. The most significant essay in the book was that by Gore himself on 'The Holy Spirit and Inspiration', in which by accepting in principle the new critical views of the Old Testament, he definitely broke with the conservative position held by Pusey and the Tractarians. Moreover, Gore went on to consider the conception of the Old Testament held by Jesus. For instance, Jesus (in Mark XII, 35–7) attributed to David a Psalm which was much later than David, probably Maccabaean. This led Gore to realize that Jesus had intellectual limitations and that the knowledge of the Old Testament possessed by later scholars was not possessed by Jesus: 'He never exhibits the omniscience of bare Godhead in the realm of natural knowledge, such as would be required to anticipate the results of modern science or criticism'.

Seldom in the history of theological controversy can a few words in a footnote have had such an effect. *Lux Mundi* in general and these words in particular caused grave offence to the older generation of Anglo-Catholics and in particular Henry Parry Liddon (1829–90), a Canon of St Paul's and a powerful preacher, who had become very prominent in the post-Tractarian stage of the movement and had hoped that Gore would make Pusey House a bastion of the old teaching in the new Oxford. Yet Broad Churchmen had already appreciated this aspect of the historic Jesus. Colenso had written:

> Lastly, it is perfectly consistent with the most entire and sincere belief in our Lord's Divinity to hold, as many do, that when He vouchsafed to become a 'Son of Man', He took our nature fully, and voluntarily entered into all the conditions of humanity, and among others, into that which makes our growth in all ordinary knowledge *gradual* and *limited*. We are expressly told in Luke II, 52, that 'Jesus increased in *wisdom*' as well as in 'stature'. It is not supposed that, in His human nature, He was acquainted, more than any educated Jew of that age, with the mysteries of all modern sciences; nor, with St Luke's expressions before us, can it be seriously maintained that as an *infant* or *young child*, He possessed a knowledge, surpassing that of the most pious and learned adults of His nation, upon the subject of the authorship and age of the different portions of the Pentateuch. At what period, then, of His life upon earth is it to be supposed that He had granted to Him, as the Son of Man, *supernaturally*, full and accurate information on these points, so that He should be expected to speak about the Pentateuch in other terms, that any other devout Jew of that day would have employed? Why

should it be thought that He would speak with certain *Divine* knowledge on this matter, more than upon other matters of ordinary science or history?

J. W. Colenso, *The Pentateuch and the Book of Joshua Critically Examined* (2 vols, 1862), vol I, xxxi–xxxii.

By the end of the nineteenth century, the successors of the Broad Churchmen, the Modernists, had started to carry the argument still further. They had begun to feel that Christ's Divinity consisted in his perfect humanity and that, therefore, Jesus differed in degree, rather than in kind, from other men. In 1895 Hastings Rashdall (1858–1924), the theologian around whom the controversy aroused by this view was later to gather, spoke these words in a sermon delivered in Balliol College Chapel, Oxford:

> If we feel that to think of God by the analogy of what is highest in the Universe is at once more rational and more reverent than to liken Him to what is lowest, or to the simply unintelligible, we must admit that in a very real sense indeed every human soul reveals God. God is in a manner reproduced in every man; so far as he is a Son of God. And in a still higher sense every good man in proportion to his goodness reveals God to his fellow-men. The highest that we know in man is the highest that we can think of God. Even a philosopher who objects to speaking of God as moral admits that he possesses something much better than morality. And what can this word 'better' mean to us but a higher degree of the goodness which we have learned to reverence in men? In Jesus Christ humanity attained its highest moral development, and just because of that perfect Humanity the conscience of mankind has recognized in Him a supreme, unique, in a sense a final revelation of that God who all through the world's history has been, by slow, successive stages, revealing Himself more and more fully to the human spirit.

Hastings Rashdall, *Doctrine and Development* (1897), 80f.

10 The Christian Socialists

The Anglo-Catholic priests, who lived and worked in the slums of the later nineteenth-century cities of England, were mostly conservative in their political outlook. They inherited from the rural Church of the eighteenth century a tradition of a hierarchical society in which each class had its divinely appointed place. John Wesley, despite his love for the common people, was no radical, while the Oxford Tractarians were typical conservatives and aristocrats, and the great revolutionary social and political changes that were taking place all over Europe were quite outside their world. Moreover, to this tradition was added the firm belief of the newly powerful Victorian middle class in *laissez-faire*: the conviction that private enterprise encouraged efficiency and initiative while state-management was likely to be corrupt and incompetent. The allegations made by Herbert Spencer (1820–1903) in the middle of the century illustrate the common outlook of the times:

> As we once heard said by a State-official of twenty-five years' standing—'Wherever there is government there is villainy.' It is the inevitable result of destroying the direct connection between the profit obtained and the work performed. No incompetent person hopes, by offering a douceur in *The Times*, to get a permanent place in a mercantile office. But where, as under government, there is no employer's self-interest to forbid—where the appointment is made by some one on whom inefficiency entails no loss; there a douceur is operative. In hospitals, in public charities, in literary funds, in endowed schools, in all social agencies in which duty done and income gained do not go hand in hand, the like corruption is found; and is great in proportion as the dependence of income upon duty is remote. In State-organisations, therefore, corruption is unavoidable. In trading organisations it rarely makes an appearance; and when it does, the instinct of self-preservation soon provides a remedy.
>
> Herbert Spencer, 'Over-Legislation', *Westminster Review* (July 1853), quoted H. V. Routh, *England Under Victoria* (1941), 197.

Such an attitude seemed to hold out little hope for the poor and especially the large property-less working-class created by the Industrial Revolution. There was not much chance of most of them being able to improve their circumstances by their own efforts. The new ideas of Socialism, originating in France, which condemned the social evils brought about by the unequal distribution of material resources and advocated some form of communal ownership of property and of the means of production and distribution, held out promises more in keeping with their needs and aspirations. In 1848 Karl Marx (1818–83), the man who did most to make Socialism a force that attracted the Continental working-classes, co-operated with another German Socialist, Frederick Engels (1820–95), in writing for a small group of German revolutionaries the *Communist Manifesto*, with its uncompromising, threatening conclusion:

> Communists scorn to hide their views and aims. They openly declare that their purposes can only be achieved by the forcible overthrow of the whole extant social order. Let the ruling classes tremble at the prospect of a communist revolution. Workers have nothing to lose but their chains. They have a world to win. WORKERS OF THE WORLD, UNITE!
>
> Quoted, L. W. Cowie, *Europe 1789–1939* (1969), 314.

Throughout Europe the year 1848 was a time of general unrest and revolt, and this stimulated a final outburst of Chartism, the English movement for political reform. It sought the fulfilment of the People's Charter, drawn up in 1838, asking for universal male suffrage, annual parliaments, voting by ballot, payment of Members of Parliament, equal electoral districts and abolition of the property qualification for Members of Parliament. A monster Chartist demonstration on Kennington Common and the presentation of a petition to Parliament was arranged for 10th April. The government was alarmed and entrusted the Duke of Wellington with the defence of the capital, but there were fewer demonstrators than expected, and the movement died of ridicule when it was discovered that the petition included numerous facetious signatures. The events of the day resulted in the following official announcement:

> In order that this people as a nation might not be wanting in general and national acknowledgement of the great disorder and jeopardy in which we are at this time placed by the machinations of the evil-disposed, and by the convulsions which agitate foreign countries, Her Majesty has directed the following Form of Prayer to ALMIGHTY GOD for the maintenance of peace and tranquillity to be offered up immediately before the General Thanksgiving, in all the Churches in

> England and Ireland on this day 'Good Friday' and on the four Sundays following . . .
>
> Quoted, Neil Stewart, *The Fight for the Charter* (1937), 229.

Not everyone in the Church of England, however, agreed with the attitude of the announcement. The Chartist fiasco of 1848 also had the effect of bringing together the three men who were to give Christian Socialism its name and being. On 10th April Charles Kingsley went up to London from his Hampshire parish of Eversley to see what was going on. He called upon his friend, Frederick Denison Maurice (1805–72), Professor of Theology at King's College, London, to discuss the situation and was introduced to a barrister, John Malcolm Forbes Ludlow (1821–1911), who had written to Maurice from Paris after the Revolution of February 1848 insisting that 'the new Socialism must be Christianized'. Two days after the Chartist meeting, when London was quiet, a few copies appeared of a placard, composed by Kingsley under the pseudonym of 'A Working Parson' and headed WORKMEN OF ENGLAND!, which concluded:

> Englishmen! Saxons! Workers of the great cool-headed, strong-handed nation of England, the workshop of the world, the leader of freedom for 700 years, men say you have commonsense! then do not humbug yourself into meaning 'license', when you cry 'liberty'. You would dare refuse you freedom? for the Almighty God, and Jesus Christ, the poor Man, who died for poor men, will bring it about for you, though all the Mammonites of the earth were against you. A nobler day is dawning for England, a day of freedom, science, industry! But there will be no true freedom without virtue, no true science without religion, no true industry without the fear of God, and love to your fellow-citizens.
>
> Workers of England, be wise, and then you *must* be free, for you will be *fit* to be free.
>
> Charles Kingsley, *op cit*, I, 118–19.

The three decided also to publish a penny journal, and the first number of *Politics for the People* came out on the 6th May 1848. It was edited by Maurice and Ludlow as a periodical devoted to considering the questions of the day, such as the franchise, taxation and the relation of capital to labour, from a viewpoint sympathetic to the poor and recognizing God's rule over mankind. Ludlow wrote more than a third of the whole, but the most outspoken contributions were by Kingsley under the pen-name of 'Parson Lot'. In the first of his 'Letters to Chartists' he sought to convince them that to end oppression and injustice a moral change was needed as much as political reform:

Suppose the Charter itself were all stuff, yet you have still a right to fair play, a patient hearing, and honourable and courteous answer, whichever way it may be. But my only quarrel with the Charter is, that it does not go far enough *in reform.* I want to set you *free*; but I do not see how what you ask for will give you what you want. I think you have fallen into just the same mistake as the rich of whom you complain—the very mistake which has been our curse and our nightmare: I mean, the mistake of fancying that legislative reform is social reform, or that men's hearts can be changed by Act of Parliament. If anyone will tell me of a country where a charter made the rogues honest, or the idle industrious, I will alter my opinion of the Charter, but not till then. It disappointed me bitterly when I read it.

Ibid, I, 146.

All the writers in *Politics for the People*, including Kingsley, upheld the idea of a class society, opposed universal suffrage and were very moderate in their descriptions of the social injustices of the time, but the journal aroused much opposition and was yet too restrained to attract working-class readers. By the end of July and the seventeenth number, it had to be abandoned for lack of support. The Christian Socialists, however, persisted in their attempts to propagate their views. In 1850 they began to publish a series of *Tracts on Christian Socialism*, which included a passionate pamphlet by Kingsley entitled *Cheap Clothes and Nasty* in which he attacked the sweated wages paid in many clothing workshops and called upon Christians not to have anything to do with them:

Tailors, who made clothing for the post-office, earned only 1s. 6d. a day, supposing them to work hard all the time, fourteen or fifteen hours. The Custom House clothing gave about the same prices. Now, all these sorts of work were performed by time workers, who, as a natural consequence of the wages they received, were the most miserable of human beings. Husband, wife, and family all worked at it; they just tried to breathe upon it; to live it never could be called. *Yet the same Government which paid such wretched wages, called upon the wretched people to be industrious, to be virtuous, and happy.* How was it possible, whatever their industry, to be virtuous and happy? The fact was, the men who, at the slack season, had been compelled to fall back upon these kinds of work, became so beggared and broken down by it, notwithstanding the assistance of their wives and families, that they were never able to rise out of it.

And now comes the question—What is to be done with these poor tailors, to the number of between fifteen and twenty thousand? Their condition, as it stands, is simply one of ever-increasing darkness and despair. The system which is ruining them is daily spreading, deepening. While we write, fresh victims are being driven by penury into the slop-working trade, fresh depreciations of labour are taking place. Like Ulysses's companions in the cave of Polyphemus, the only question among them is, to scramble so far back as to have *a chance of being eaten at last.* Before them is ever-nearing slavery, disease, and starvation. What can be done?

First—this can be done. That no man who calls himself a Christian—no man who calls himself a man—shall ever disgrace himself by dealing at any show-shop or slop-shop. It is easy enough to know them.

Charles Kingsley, *Cheap Clothes and Nasty* (1850), in A. C. Ward (ed), *Tracts and Pamphlets* (1927), 533.

Kingsley went on in this pamphlet also to call upon people to support the Society of Promoters which the Christian Socialists founded to run co-operative workshops in London for tailoring, printing, baking and other crafts. These workshops only lasted for a short time, being supported mainly by the early converts to Christian Socialism who became known by their 'strange-patterned and ill-fitting trousers'. More successful among the efforts of the Christian Socialists were their evening classes, which gradually developed into the Working Mens' College, a centre established in Great Ormond Street in 1854. The prime mover in the establishment of the College was Maurice, who in the previous year had been compelled to resign from his professorship at King's College because he had attacked the popular view of the endlessness of future punishment and maintained that in the New Testament 'eternity' had nothing to do with time. Maurice was, indeed, the most important and influential of the group because his Christian Socialism was rooted explicitly in theology. He stated that for him real Christianity or Church Reformation involved:

theologically the reassertion of God's Absolute, Fatherly Love, the Incarnation, the Sacrifice for all, in their fullness, apart from their Calvinistic or Tractarian limitations or dilutions; *socially* the assertion of an actual living community under Christ, in which no man has a right to call anything that he has his own but in which there is spiritual fellowship and practical co-operation; *nationally* the assertion of a union, grounded not on alliances and compromises but on the constitution of things, between this Universal Community and the State, of which the principle is Personal Distinction and the symbol Property. For this I desire to labour in all ways, being most careful to choose none by self-will or from mere calculations of expediency, and to avoid none which God points out, because it may seem dangerous to oneself or to mere formal onlookers. I believe whoever enters on this path must lay his account with opposition, active or passive, from all quarters, must eagerly welcome and set down for gain all tokens of sympathy; must have no confidence in himself; must cultivate entire confidence in God and in the certainty of His purposes. It will and must be a long battle, in which many, even standard-bearers, will fall. But the issue is not to be doubted; let us work and trust for it.

Frederick Maurice, *Life and Letters of F. D. Maurice* (2 vols, 1884), II, 9–10.

As the leader of the Christian Socialist movement, who sought to express its purpose in terms of Christian philosophy, Maurice was not the man to give himself to political programmes of action. In the name of theology he was opposed to the whole *laissez-faire*, competitive, commercialist outlook. Men, he insisted, as created by God and redeemed by Christ, were not bound to compete with each other in selfish self-interest, but rather they realized their true purpose by co-operating as children of God and brothers in Christ. By 'Socialism' he meant the working out of a structure of society which would enable men to strive with one another instead of against one another, and by 'Christian Socialism' he meant that this would have to be based upon Christian inspiration and ideas; but he did not think that this involved state intervention and organization, and he did not adopt any particular economic doctrine:

Christian socialism is to my mind, the assertion of God's order. Every attempt to hide it under a great machinery, call it Organization of Labour, Central Board, or what you like, I must protest against as hindering the gradual development of what I regard as a divine purpose, as an attempt to create a new constitution of society, when what we want is that the old constitution should exhibit its true functions and energies.

Ibid, II, 44.

Maurice's outlook helped to make Christian Socialism acceptable to some church-people, but to most its association with the Chartists and other reformers made it dangerously suspect. The prevailing temper in England at that time was uncompromisingly hostile to such a development in the Church. One of the most bitter attacks on the Christian Socialists was made in an article by John Wilson Croker (1780–1857), the originator of the term Conservative and the enemy of Lord Macaulay (who 'detested him more than cold boiled veal'). Making use of a well-known controversial device, he referred to various Socialist views, which he alleged included the advocacy of murder, the abolition of private property and the denegation of marriage, and then turned to the Christian Socialists:

> Incredible as it may appear, there is, it seems, a clique of educated and clever, but wayward-minded men—the most prominent of them two *clergymen of the Church of England*—who from, as it seems, a morbid craving for notoriety or a crazy straining after paradox, have taken up the unnatural and unhallowed task of preaching, in the press and from the pulpit, not indeed such open, undisguised *Jacobinism* and *Jacquerie* as we have just been quoting, but under the name of '*Christian Socialism*,' the same doctrines in a form not the less dangerous for being less honest. . . . It certainly adds to our surprise to find the reputed editor of 'Politics for the People' and the avowed author of other works, theological as well as political, of a still more heterodox character, occupying the professorial chair of Divinity at *King's College, London.*
>
> *Quarterly Review*, LXXXIX (1851), 524.

By the middle of the 1850s the Christian Socialist movement had failed, partly because of the hostility of churchpeople and the indifference of the working-class itself and partly because of the absorption of public interest in the Crimean War (1854–56). Its three leaders had to abandon their efforts on its behalf, though their work was not to be without effect. There remained individuals who were strongly influenced by their ideas and were stirred to put them into practice in later years. One of these, for instance, was Octavia Hill (1838–1912), the housing reformer, who in 1875 wrote in a letter to Ludlow:

> It remains true that it was the early connection with that body of Christian Socialists to which much of my present work must owe its spirit. It had to find its own form, according to the needs and possibilities of circumstances, but its spirit must have been influenced deeply by the deeds and words of all that group of men, among whom it pleased God to lead me, when life was just first presenting its puzzles to me.
>
> E. Moberly Bell, *Octavia Hill* (1942), 24.

Nevertheless, for some twenty years after the collapse of the Christian Socialist movement, there was no organized group within the Church of England that concerned itself with the social implications of the Christian religion. In that period a growing number of the new generation of Anglo-Catholic clergymen went to work in slum parishes, but it was not until 1877 that they began to organize themselves in the cause of social reform. In that year the Guild of St Matthew was founded in the parish of St Matthew, Bethnal Green, by a young priest, Stewart Headlam (1847–1924), who was then its Vicar. Headlam had derived from the theology of Maurice a concern for social righteousness that went beyond the original Tractarian tradition. The Guild consisted entirely of communicants, and its objects were:

> (i) To get rid, by every possible means, of the existing prejudices, especially on the part of Secularists, against the Church, her sacraments and doctrines, and to endeavour to 'justify God to the people'.
>
> (ii) To promote frequent and reverent worship in the Holy Communion, and a better observance of the teaching of the Church of England, as set forth in the Book of Common Prayer.
>
> (iii) To promote the study of social and political questions in the light of the Incarnation.
>
> F. G. Bettany, *Stewart Headlam* (1926), 79–80.

The Guild of St Matthew had no existence apart from its leader. Its programme was an unusual combination of his personal crusades, and he was often in trouble with the bishops, whether for practising extreme ritualism, attacking conventional teaching about everlasting punishment or championing the wearing of short skirts and flesh-coloured tights by ballet-girls on the stage. He also urged such objects as the nationalization of the land, a progressive income tax, universal suffrage and the abolition of the House of Lords. The Guild never had a membership of more than a few hundred, though it included some prominent churchmen. Headlam thought that its most flourishing time was round about 1884, the year when it held an open-air public demonstration in Trafalgar Square and passed a resolution in favour of thoroughgoing State Socialism:

> Whereas the present contrast between the great body of the workers who produce much and consume little, and of those classes who produce little and consume much is contrary to the Christian doctrines of brotherhood and justice, this meeting urges on all Churchmen the duty of supporting such measures as will tend—(a) To restore to the people the value which they gave to the land; (b) to bring about a better distribution of the wealth created by labour; (c) to give the whole body of the people a voice in their own government; (d) to abolish false standards of worth and dignity.
>
> *Ibid*, 83.

Headlam's radical social principles and involvement in multifarious controversies gained him the reputation of a wild man and put off some churchpeople who otherwise might have supported the Guild, which began to decline in the 1890s and was dissolved in 1909. Its decline was hastened by the foundation of the Christian Social Union which grew at its expense. The Christian Social Union was founded in 1889, the year of the appearance of *Lux Mundi,* and it originated with the same group of men who were the contributors to this book. Gore was one of its most active members and influential leaders, and Westcott was its first President. Henry Scott Holland (1847–1918), another contributor to *Lux Mundi,* was its first Secretary. He was both a Liberal Catholic in religion and a Liberal in politics, keenly interested in relating Christian principles to the social and economic problems of living:

> Why is it that this Church of ours ... so rich in her Catholic inheritance, so interwoven into England's story ... should somehow appear to the masses of English workers in country and in town now at the very crisis of their fate, as if she stood aloof from their very life, and was cold to their aspirations and suspicious of their aims and helpless in their needs; why should she wear the aspect to them of something privileged and propertied, jealous and timid, and carry with her so little of the likeness of Christ?
>
> H. S. Holland, 'National Penitence', *Lombard Street in Lent* (1894), 9.

As a canon of St Paul's from 1884 to 1910, Scott Holland was an influential preacher, and the Christian Social Union found in him its most brilliant spokesman and exponent of its objects which were declared to be:

> (i) To claim for the Christian Law the ultimate authority to rule social practice.
>
> (ii) To study in common how to apply the moral truths and principles of Christianity to the social and economic difficulties of the present time.
>
> (iii) To present Christ in practical life as the Living Master and King, the enemy of wrong and selfishness, the power of righteousness and love.
>
> L. Elliott Binns, *Religion in the Victorian Era* (1936), 268.

A comparison of its objectives with those of the Guild of St Matthew shows its different purpose. Instead of political propaganda and outspoken denunciations, its aim was rather research and education. It wished to establish the principle that the Christian religion was concerned with the whole ordering of the life of man in society and to consider the implications of this by organizing study groups. This did not mean, however, that it refrained from any form of political action. In some ways it went back to the methods of the first Christian Socialists. In addition to its literature and meetings, it compiled 'white lists' of approved traders, denounced instances of bad wages and overwork and examined the conditions in dangerous trades. Harold Anson, later Master of the Temple, who took his degree at Oxford in 1889 and stayed up to read theology in preparation for ordination, wrote of those early days of the Christian Social Union:

> I joined at this time the newly formed 'Christian Social Union', which aimed at bringing home to the Church its responsibility for the material and social conditions of the nation. It was really a new view, even a revolutionary view, in Church circles, that a profession of Churchmanship involved a responsibility for social conditions. This had indeed been preached by Maurice and Kingsley and by some of the Broad Church divines, but had never penetrated far into the conscience of the Church as a whole. Our task was to drive into the Church's conscience the truth that baptism meant nothing if it did not mean initiation into a society which was leading an active Christian life in the world, and that receiving Communion was a mockery if it did not mean sharing your bread and wine (i.e. your land and houses and education) with your fellow-Christians. So we were taught to scan anxiously our sources of wealth, if we had any. The rich squire was told that it was not enough that he supported the Church, or even that he was a model landlord. 'How about those "Great Western" shares of yours? Have you ever been to Swindon, and seen how your porters and engine-drivers live from whose labours you keep up your village?'
>
> The model Churchwoman was asked whether she was aware that the people who made her cups and saucers suffered tortures from lead poisoning. Why was she not using leadless glaze? (I have now some crockery which refuses to be broken, which I bought some thirty years ago in a passion for using nothing in my home but leadless china.) Bishops were urged to have their gaiters and aprons made by co-operative tailors, who, incidentally, made their clothing very badly. Deans and Chapters had it pointed out to them that they battened on slums. We were all made to feel that we were little short of infidels, and that it made it much worse that we went regularly to Communion, and yet denied in our daily lives that it is in the meat and drink of life that the Real Presence is found and not in visions of angels and saints in the clouds. No wonder that we got very unpopular.
>
> Harold Anson, *Looking Forward* (1938), 120–1.

By 1900 the Christian Social Union had nearly fifty branches and over 4,000 members of whom nearly 1,500 were clergymen. It was, therefore, much larger and also more influential than previous social movements in the Church of England. It had, however, its weaknesses. Taking the Church as a whole, its membership was small, and it had no more success in attracting working-class members than the other organizations. In addition, it suffered continually from disunity, particularly because of disagreement between those who were Socialists (in the political sense of the word) and those who were not. This tended to make its pronouncements sometimes vague and indefinite and hindered its efforts to influence the Church. James Adderley, one of the Socialist members, was disappointed that the bishops of the whole Anglican communion, who met for the Lambeth Conference of 1897, had not been persuaded to choose more definite social subjects for their agenda:

> It is disappointing to find only two very 'safe' social subjects placed on the agenda, 'The unemployed' and 'Co-operation'. Surely if the Bishops wished to deal with these matters they should have selected serious moral questions, such as '*Commercial Morality*', '*Sweating*'. Of course these questions might bring us into conflict with the average plutocrat who subscribes to our Church expenses. But are we afraid of him? God help us if we are! What a glorious thing a really courageous Lambeth Conference would be.
>
> James Adderley, *Goodwill* (October 1896), 223.

Nevertheless, the Christian Social Union did achieve considerable results. It was strongest in the universities, especially Oxford, so that it was in a position to influence the future leaders of both Church and State. For the Church it meant that the clergy who now went into the slum parishes adopted a wider and more aggressive attitude towards the causes and consequences of the poverty and suffering they saw around them. A clergyman later said of his experience at Jarrow, where he became an incumbent in 1897:

> I came to the conclusion that, as a member of the Christian Social Union, my first urgent task was to blazon abroad the nature of the housing conditions in St Peter's parish, and the shameful evils to moral and physical health to which they inevitably lead.
>
> K. S. Inglis, *Churches and the Working Classes in Victorian England* (1963), 281.

Perhaps the most important single person to be influenced by the Christian Social Union was William Temple, who, while a young fellow of Queen's College, Oxford, and not yet ordained, helped in the organization of a Sweated Industries Exhibition in

1907 which displayed the results of *laissez-faire* in the industrial system. In the handbook to the Exhibition he wrote:

> It is the system which is foul and rotten. Producer, capitalist, consumer—all are entangled in the meshes of its net. While we prate about the spread of refinement; and while we pride ourselves on the spread of education; while we glory in an Empire whose Flag is said to stand for Justice—we are convicted by the facts at our own doors, of stupid coarseness, of ignorant insensibility, and of wanton oppression. We form Army Corps, we build 'Dreadnoughts'; we discuss endlessly what metaphysics are to be taught to children in our schools. But if we listen, there is still the desolate cry of the Son of Man: 'I am hungry and ye give me no meat.'
>
> F. A. Iremonger, *William Temple, Archbishop of Canterbury* (1948), 329.

At least the Christian Social Union, following the trail opened up by Maurice and the other founders of the first Christian Socialist movement, did a great deal to make churchpeople see something of what responsibility for social justice involved. And Temple was to be an important leader in the twentieth century in ensuring that Christian social thinking gained a realistic perception of this issue.

The Christian Social Union had an effect also on the opinion of those outside the Church of England. The idea that the Church represented the wealthier classes and was indifferent to the social problems of the time long persisted, but the Christian Social Union began to correct this impression. A report in a local newspaper of one of its meetings in the Albert Hall, Leeds, at the end of the century stated:

> Because it [the Church of England] has been a favoured and a greatly privileged religious community, its Bishops and clergy and members have laboured to maintain privilege and to perpetuate injustice . . . But here is the Christian Social Union professing principles that can only be heartily welcomed if they are the means of breaking down the resistance of the State Church to certain necessary measures of social reform . . . If the Church of England with all its resources and agencies could throw its influence into the scale against some of the crying evils of our time, reformers would cease to stand almost in despair before the difficulties that confront them.
>
> *Leeds Mercury*, 27th November 1900.

11 The Missionaries

Although in the seventeenth and eighteenth centuries England had become an important commercial nation with an increasing overseas empire in non-Christian parts of the world, she was slow in accepting any religious responsibility towards their peoples. The Society for Promoting Christian Knowledge, founded in 1699, tried to send English missionaries to work among the natives in the East India Company's settlements, but without success. Henry Newman (1670–1743), the Secretary of the Society, wrote in 1713 to Thomas Wilson, Bishop of Sodor and Man:

> [The Society] has long been endeavouring to find out fit persons for so great a work, but has not yet met with any who are both sufficiently qualified and also willing and at liberty to undertake it. They would gladly have men of a sober and religious conversation, endowed with a meek and humble spirit, men pretty well mortified and dead to the world and worldly advantages, of some experience in the care of souls and zealous for the glory of God and the salvation of men. If with these divine qualities, they have learning and an aptitude to learn languages, it will be a great advantage.
>
> L. W. Cowie, *Henry Newman* (1956), 114.

In the event, since no English clergymen were prepared to go to India as missionaries, the Society during the eighteenth and early nineteenth centuries had to be content with appointing and supporting Lutheran missionaries from Germany and Scandinavia to work in the Company's territory. It was through the influence of the religious revival fostered by the Methodists and Evangelicals that a new impetus was given to overseas missionary effort. The story began with the establishment of the Particular Baptist Society for the Propagation of the Gospel among the Heathen in 1792 by a small group of Baptist preachers in the little back parlour of a house in Kettering. Its foundation was in a large measure due to the earnest pleading of William Carey (1761–1834), a Northamptonshire cobbler who had become a part-time pastor and wrote in 1792 a pamphlet entitled *An Enquiry into the Obligation of Christians to use Means for the Conversion of the Heathens.* In one section he dealt with certain common excuses that were made in opposition to missionary work, such as:

> As to their [the heathen] uncivilised and barbarous way of living, this can be no objection to any, except those whose love of ease renders them unwilling to expose themselves to inconveniences for the good of others. It was no objection to the apostles and their successors, who went among the barbarous Germans and Gauls, and still more barbarous Britons! They did not wait for the ancient inhabitants of these countries to become civilised before they could be christianised, but went simply with the doctrine of the cross; and Tertullian could boast that 'those parts of Britain which were proof against the Roman armies, were conquered by the gospel of Christ'. It was no objection to an Eliot or a Brainerd in later times. They went forth, and encountered every difficulty of the kind, and found that a cordial reception of the gospel produced those happy effects which the longest intercourse with Europeans without it could never accomplish. It *is* no objection to commercial men. It only requires that we should have as much love to the souls of our fellow-creatures and fellow-sinners, as they have from the profits arising from a few otter-skins, and all these difficulties would be easily surmounted.
>
> George Smith, *The Life of William Carey* (1935), 25.

In 1793 Carey went to India as the Society's first missionary. His *Enquiry* played an important part also in the formation of the London Missionary Society in 1795 by a body of Congregationalists, Anglicans, Presbyterians and Methodists, who combined to promote Christian missions to the heathen and sent out the first twenty-nine missionaries under its auspices to Tahiti in the next year. Its Directors adopted a declaration in 1796 declaring that one of its principles was that individual missionaries should be left free to choose whatever form of Church government they held right:

> As the union of God's people of various Denominations, in carrying on this great Work, is a most desirable Object, so, to prevent, if possible, any cause of future dissension, it is declared to be a fundamental principle of the Missionary Society, that our design is not to send Presbyterianism, Independency, Episcopacy or any other form of Church Order or Government (about which there may be differences of opinion among serious Persons), but the Glorious Gospel of the blessed God to the Heathen: and that it shall be left (as it ever

> ought to be left) to the minds of the Persons whom God may call into the fellowship of His Son from among them to assume for themselves such form of Church Government as to them shall appear most agreeable to the Word of God.
>
> E. A. Payne, *The Growth of the World Church* (1955), 79–80.

In the event, however, the London Missionary Society came to be supported almost exclusively by the Congregationalists. Carey himself had said in his *Enquiry* that 'in the present divided state of Christendom, it would be more likely for good to be done by each denomination engaging separately in the work, than if they were to embark upon it conjointly'. Many Evangelicals, especially those who held responsible positions in Church or State, did not consider themselves able to support anything but an exclusively Anglican society, and in 1799 the Church Missionary Society was founded (see p. 16). The Society was pledged to uphold episcopal order, but its purpose was thought essentially to be the proclamation of the news of the saving life and death of Christ. Thomas Haweis (1734–1820), Rector of Aldwinkle, Northamptonshire, defined in a sermon the Evangelical conception of the missionary message:

> We appeal to the experience of all ages, what ever did, or ever can control the unruly wills and affections of sinful men, but the preaching the Cross of our Lord Jesus Christ: by whom, saith St Paul, *the world is crucified unto me, and I unto the world.* Without this, what could a missionary effect in a heathen land? How poor, how unavailing would be all the weapons of vain philosophy and false Christianity! *Embelle telum sine ictu.* Brethren, our whole success will depend upon this one point; if Christ be preached—only preached, always preached—then shall we see the power of His death and resurrection, and the Lord will add again *daily to His church of such as shall be saved.*
>
> Quoted, R. Lovett, *A Primer of Modern Missions* (1896), 29.

Another effect of the Evangelical revival, which had important consequences for missionary work in India, was a change in the character of the chaplains sent out by the East India Company, who had hitherto been few in number and made little attempt to establish contact with the native peoples. The change was particularly due to the influence of Charles Simeon, who sent out his disciples to be 'princes in all lands', and by far the most notable of these new 'pious chaplains' was Henry Martyn, who arrived in Calcutta in 1806 and died in Persia on his way home to England in 1813, at the age of thirty-one. A Fellow of St John's College, Cambridge, he not only worked as a missionary, but also translated the New Testament into Hindustani and Persian, the

Psalms into Persian and the Book of Common Prayer into Hindustani, besides preparing a translation of the New Testament into Arabic. His life of devotion to the cause of missions made a great impression at home. Simeon always had a portrait of him hanging over the fireplace in his dining-room:

> He used often to look at it in his friends' presence, and to say, as he did so, with a peculiar loving emphasis, 'There, see that blessed man! What an expression of countenance! No one looks at me as he does; he never takes his eyes off me, and seems always to be saying, "Be serious—be in earnest—don't trifle."' Then smiling at the picture and gently bowing, he would add, 'And I won't trifle—I won't trifle.'
>
> H. C. G. Moule, *Charles Simeon* (1892), 140.

As Anglican missionary work developed, bishops were appointed to overseas territories, but it was an indication of the lukewarm attitude towards foreign missions in official ecclesiastical circles that the consecration of these first bishops took place semi-privately in the seclusion of Lambeth Palace Chapel; and when Reginald Heber was consecrated Bishop of Calcutta in 1823, it was regarded as a considerable concession that Mrs Heber was allowed to bring two friends to the service. After the consecration of George Augustus Selwyn as the first Bishop of New Zealand in 1841, however, a friend, Edward Coleridge, protested strongly at the nature of the service, with the result that in 1847 one South African and three Australian bishops were consecrated at a service in Westminster Abbey at which there were 760 communicants:

> I could not help feeling that we ought to have been thousands rather than ten, gathered together as with one consent in St Paul's or Westminster Abbey, to witness the sending out by the Church of the first Bishop of the appointment, and not as we were, a few persons in an upper chamber—as if we were afraid or ashamed of that great deed which we came to sanction by our presence and our prayers. It is an actual fact that my own cousin, the present Bishop of Barbados, was admitted to that sacred office in the presence of only two persons besides the necessary attendants. Such cannot last much longer. The feeling of the Church will become so strong and the cry of indignation so loud that it will pierce even the walls of Addington and so rouse the Archbishop from his slumbers.
>
> Quoted, J. McLeod Campbell, *Christian History in the Making* (1946), 113–14.

Selwyn remained in New Zealand until 1868, able and determined, tireless and devout. The Maoris rapidly adopted Christianity, most of them becoming Anglicans, but other missions were at work among them as well. A book, describing the circumstances of the colony in 1850, spoke of the religious situation there in matter-of-fact terms:

> Quite three-fourths of the New Zealanders [i.e. Maoris] are now missionary converts, perhaps in the proportion of one Roman Catholic to four Wesleyans

Missionaries arriving in New Zealand

> and eight Churchmen . . . How much, or how little, of this may be Christianity; how much, or how little, of it may arise from the circumstance of the new religion being the *fashion*, and a passport to the rich missionary countries of blankets and tobacco, it is impossible to say—nor should we care to ask. Whites as well as blacks may pray because it pays to pray; and if, by calling himself Peter and going to chapel in a beaver hat, the Maori is likely (as is the case) to become a better customer and a better man, surely his doing so is a gain to the community and no loss to himself.
>
> C. Hursthouse, *New Zealand* (2 vols, 1857), I, 164.

Even, however, after official support had been gained at home for the missionary cause, and gains were being made in overseas lands, there was as yet little enthusiasm among most churchpeople. When G. H. Wilkinson became Vicar of Seaham Harbour in 1859, he was very anxious to secure interest and support for overseas missions in the parish. Many years later he described to his daughter the result of his efforts:

> As time went on, I thought I would have a missionary meeting. I planned it out very keenly, put up posters in every direction and expected great things. After all, only the schoolmaster and his wife and father and mother were present. I made them sit down, and I gave the address and had all the prayers as if there was a large congregation, and ten shillings was collected.
>
> A. J. Mason, *op cit*, 25.

The failure of this effort was all the more marked because Wilkinson had established Bible-classes which were well-attended by the working-men of the parish. Yet by then the tide had already begun to turn. David Livingstone (1813–73) was catching the public imagination and kindling its enthusiasm for overseas missions. He had embarked in 1840 for the Cape of Good Hope to begin his work as a missionary in the Bechuana country. Reports of his explorations and experiences began to arouse interest in England, and when he returned in 1856 he was received with growing enthusiasm. In 1857 he published his *Missionary Travels and Researches in South Africa*, the first edition of twelve thousand copies at a guinea each being sold out before publication. In it he expounded his theme of 'Christianity and Commerce' which he believed would destroy the terrible slave-trade and open up Africa to civilization:

> Commerce breaks up the sullen isolations of heathenism. It is so far good, though Christianity also reaches the very centre of the wants of Africa and of the world. Here is a most desirable central point for the spread of civilisation and Christianity ... If the movement now begun is not checked by some untoward event, the slave-trade will certainly come to a natural termination in this quarter.
>
> J. McLeod Campbell, *op cit*, 133–4.

The result of Livingstone's appeals (and especially one he made in the Senate House at Cambridge in 1857) was the formation of the Universities' Mission to Central Africa in 1859, and another appeal in 1875 by the explorer, H. M. Stanley (1841–1904), led the Church Missionary Society to begin work in Uganda. By an Anglo-German agreement of 1887 Uganda was recognized as within the British sphere, and in 1890 the British East Africa Company began operations there, but by 1894 it had reached the end of its financial resources and announced that it must cease to administer the country. The massacre of Christians and the revival of the slave trade was threatened. By now, however, the British public had been aroused by the examples of the missionaries from indifference to the fate of Africa. Opinion was vocal, and the government had to act. The new Foreign Secretary, Lord Rosebery, made it a condition of accepting office in Gladstone's ministry that Uganda should be made a British protectorate:

> 'Continuity of moral policy is a moral force by which in my opinion this country has to be judged. It is the salt which savours our history; it is a spirit which has exalted it and it is by that when we have passed away that in my belief we shall come to be judged. As Greece is best remembered by her literature, Rome by her laws, so this country, when this country stands before history, will stand not by her fleets or her armies or her commerce but by her heroic self-denying exertions which she has put forward to put down this iniquitous traffic.'
>
> *Ibid*, 145.

That the British government had been compelled to adopt a moral attitude towards its responsibilities in Uganda was largely due to Alexander Mackay (1849–90), 'Mackay of the Great Lake', a skilled Scottish engineer who was accepted by the Church Missionary Society for their new mission in Uganda and reached the shore of Lake Nyanza in 1878. He spent the rest of his life in Uganda, enduring hardship and danger, the martyrdom of his converts and the death of two bishops sent to help him, one being murdered and the other dying of sickness, and yet he continued without thought of giving up, and he gained great influence over the native Baganda. After he had spent only two of his fourteen years in Africa, he said:

> It is no sacrifice, as some think, to come here as pioneers of Christianity and of civilisation. I would not give my position here for all the world. A powerful race has to be won from darkness to light; superstition and idolatry have to be overthrown; men have to be taught to love God and love their neighbour, which means the uprooting of institutions that have lasted for centuries; labour made noble, the slave set free, knowledge imparted, and wisdom implanted; and, above all, that true wisdom taught which alone can elevate man from a brute to a son of God. Who would not willingly engage in such noble work, and consider it the highest honour on earth to be called to do it?
>
> S. C. Carpenter, *Church and People*, 455.

The missionary societies themselves were generally in favour of the extension of British rule overseas, not only because it was on the whole animated by moral ideals to which they subscribed, but also because it ensured freedom for their own work. The British government did not give support in the colonies to any policy of Christianization, but its insistence upon toleration and absence of religious discrimination was advantageous to both native creeds and missionary evangelization. Thus, Queen Victoria's proclamation in 1858, when the Crown took over the administration of India, was primarily intended to restore the confidence of Hindus and Moslems, but it also ensured the deliverance of missionaries from the hostile prejudices and discrimination from which they had suffered under the East India Company:

> *Firmly relying ourselves on the truth of Christianity, and acknowledging with gratitude the solace of religion,* We disclaim alike the right and desire to impose Our convictions on any of Our subjects. We declare it to be Our royal will and pleasure that none be in anywise favoured, none molested or disquieted by reason of their religious faith or observance, but that all alike shall enjoy the equal and impartial protection of the law . . . And it is Our further will that, so far as may be, Our subjects, of whatever race or creed, be freely and impartially admitted to offices in Our service, the duties of which they may be qualified by their education, ability and integrity, duly to discharge.
>
> Stephen Neil, *A History of Christian Missions* (Pelican History of the Church, vol VI, 1964), 323.

Queen Victoria herself added the opening words in italics to the original draft of the proclamation, and the missions inevitably enjoyed considerable prestige as representing the religion professed by the colonial governors. Nor was it possible for the authorities to be, in fact, completely neutral towards the work of the missions. And in one particular way the colonial administration assisted them. It became increasingly common for such administrations to give financial assistance to missionary hospitals and schools. In India this began as early as 1854, when the government set forth an Educational Despatch in which it declared it would give grants-in-aid to mission schools, which would have to accept government inspection and guidance, but remain free to give such religious instruction to their pupils as they wished. Sir Charles Wood, the grandfather of Lord Irwin, a later Viceroy, in defending the arrangements in a famous speech in the House of Commons, remarked:

> I believe that by doing so we shall not weaken but strengthen our empire. But even if the reverse should be the case—even if the result should be the loss of empire—it seems to me that this country will occupy a far better and prouder

> position in the history of the world, if by our agency a civilized and Christian empire should be established in India, than if we continue to rule over a people debased by ignorance and degraded by superstition.
>
> *Ibid*, 357.

As the activities of the missions increased, so they had to develop special organizations to carry them out. To educational and medical work, there was added work among women. At first this was pioneered by wives who accompanied their missionary husbands, and there was a prejudice against sending out single-women missionaries. As late as 1842, Daniel Wilson (1778–1858), Bishop of Calcutta, wrote that he objected 'on principle' to an unmarried woman being sent out to India:

> I imagine the beloved Persis, Tryphena and Tryphosa, Julia, Nereus and his sister, and others who 'laboured much in the Lord', remained in their own neighbourhoods and families, and that no unmarried female would have thought of a voyage of fourteen thousand miles to find out a scene of duty. The whole thing is against the Apostolic maxim, 'I suffer not a woman to speak in the Church'.
>
> P. L. Garlick, 'A Century of Progress in Women's Work', *The Church Overseas*, July 1934.

It was not long, however, before suspicion and hostility were broken down, and many women missionaries went overseas. In some Anglican missions, work among women was undertaken by members of sisterhoods, and the English sisterhoods established a growing number of overseas houses. An argument in favour of the particular value of sisterhoods in the mission field was that their ideals of poverty, humility and service represented the complete sacrifice in following Christ that did away with all distinctions of race and colour. When Frank Weston was Bishop of Zanzibar from 1908 to 1930, he founded in 1910 the Community of the Sacred Passion to work in his diocese. He told its members in a letter:

> What we are bound to aim at is such a level of fellowship (with Africans) as will convince the people that Christianity is not a religion for white people and their dependants, but a religion of actual fellowship between race and race, and colour and colour.
>
> H. Maynard Smith, *Frank, Bishop of Zanzibar* (1926), 137.

Missionary work was also undertaken by Anglican religious communities for men, which were, however, slower in developing than the sisterhoods. Among these was the Society of the Sacred Mission, originally founded as the Korean Missionary

Brotherhood by Herbert Kelly in 1890 with the object of training men for work in Korea. His description of its beginnings in a rented 'ugly house at Brixton', where he and three other men studied with the aid of local curates as tutors, reveals an amazing austerity combined with a picnic-like existence:

> We furnished the house in our own fashion—wooden chairs, deal tables, iron beds and cooking irons. We had a small room for an oratory. I will describe our life at once, for it changed little for many years. We began with Prime and Mattins at six, and after a short interval—time enough to do our rooms—we went to the Celebration in Church at 7 a.m. Thence back to breakfast, which we managed ourselves. It was a plain bread and butter breakfast, with jam, I admit. Then began the housework. One man was responsible for accounts, one for washing up, and one swept the stairs. They changed round monthly. At 9 a.m. we had Terce, and then worked till dinner at 1.30 p.m. with Sext at 12 noon. None was at 2 p.m., tea at 6 p.m.—bread and butter as before. Evensong in Church at 7 p.m., and Compline at 9.30 p.m. Silence was kept till Sext next day. It was years after—I forget how long—before we learnt to divide the silence into a Greater, or absolute silence, up to Terce, and a Lesser, from all talk other than about work, up to Sext. It was not a very well organized day, but we managed. Saturday was scrubbing day. Canon Brooke found us a most delightful old lady, Mrs Staples, a true servant of God, who would come and cook for us.
>
> Herbert Kelly, *No Pious Person* (1960), 46.

Anglican overseas missions faced particular problems through the established position of the Church of England. At first bishops appointed to colonial dioceses exercised their jurisdiction by virtue of Letters Patent issued by the Crown, but as the colonies became self-governing their position had to be reconsidered. The complicated dispute between Colenso and Gray made it clear that a Church in a self-governing colony could not in any sense be legally a part of the Church of England. The Judicial Committee of the Privy Council in 1863 delivered this judgment in another South African case:

> The Church of England, in places where there is no church established by law [i.e. in colonies with legislative bodies of their own, such as Cape Colony had become in 1852] is in the same situation with any other religious body, in no better, but in no worse position, and the members may adopt ... rules for enforcing discipline within their body, which will be binding on those who expressly or by implication have assented to them ... in such cases the tribunals

> so constituted are not in any sense courts; they derive no authority from the Crown, they have no power of their own to enforce their sentences.
>
> Stephen Neil, *Anglicanism* (1958), 305–6.

An important consequence of this situation was that it became essential for each of the different overseas Churches of the Anglican communion to devise its own form of self-government. In 1850 Selwyn received from the Governor, the Chief Justice and many other prominent laymen in New Zealand a statement of their

> earnest conviction that a peculiar necessity exists for the speedy establishment of some system of Church government amongst us, which by assigning to each order in the Church its appropriate duties might call forth the energies of all, and thus enable the whole body of the Church most efficiently to perform its functions . . . promote God's service, spread wide a knowledge of the Gospel, and secure the welfare of those vast numbers of our fellow-countrymen who must hereafter occupy these islands.
>
> H. W. Tucker, *Life of George Augustus Selwyn* (2 vols, 1879), II, 90.

Selwyn exercised his strong ruling capacity to bring back the Church in New Zealand from the semi-presbyterianism of the individualistic, Evangelical missionaries, who had converted the Maoris, to control by a powerful General Synod on which the laity were represented. That Churches should develop along their own lines was even more important in countries which had no connections of race or sentiment with England. By the end of the nineteenth century it was being increasingly realized that the aim of missionary work must be to establish, in the words of Archbishop Benson, 'true Native Churches'. He elaborated on this point in a letter to Edward Bickersteth, who was Bishop of Tokyo from 1886 to 1897:

> This becomes of course much plainer and much easier of execution when we and our clergy remember that the great end of our planting a Church in Japan is that there may be a *Japanese* Church, not an English Church. Any forgetfulness of this, any aiming at a different end, will only reproduce in the next 100 years the miseries which have arisen from the Italian Church in the days of her prosperity having determined to be the Church of other lands.
>
> A. C. Benson, *Edward White Benson* (1 vol ed, 1901, 460).

The efforts of the English missionary societies during these years contributed to the world-wide growth of Christianity which was unprecedented in any other age.

A missionary in China

Often people, who were wearied by the religious disputations and narrowness at home, turned with relief to the great opportunities existing overseas, and the period ended with an incident that showed the conflict produced in the mission field by the conflict between those who wished to preserve their traditional loyalties and those who sought to break away from them. In 1913 the Bishops of Mombasa and Uganda, dioceses supported by the Church Missionary Society, instituted at Kikuyu, a village in British East Africa, a missionary conference of Anglicans, Presbyterians and other Protestants, who proposed that their Churches should form a federation and ended their proceedings with a united Communion service. This scandalized Bishop Weston of Zanzibar, who was a strong Anglo-Catholic, and he issued a pamphlet against it:

> Easier were it to receive in brotherly love all who seek fellowship with us, honouring their principles as we honour their lives and labours. But He Who came to send a sword upon the earth will not have it so. Rather must we drink of His cup, and true to principle however unpopular and seemingly destined to bring failure in its train, we must be content to become the scorn of men and the outcasts of the people.
>
> For, whatever else may be said about reunion and the methods of attaining it, one thing is above all else true: without principle we shall accomplish nothing. And since the movement which produced the Kijuyu Conference is evidently at fault in the matter of principles, it is necessary to move backwards and return to prayer and study.

H. Maynard Smith, *op cit*, 159.

Weston also appealed to the Archbishop of Canterbury, Randall Davidson, who made a statement in terms which meant, according to a satirical contemporary interpretation, 'What took place at Kikuyu was most well-pleasing to God, but must never be allowed to recur.' A letter written to *The Times* by Hensley Henson, then Dean of Durham, made it clear that the affair raised issues which, though felt most starkly in the mission field, were of much wider consequence. After asserting that great English Churchmen in the past had both admitted non-episcopalians to Communion and themselves received the Sacrament from non-episcopalian ministers, he stated:

> It is true that the position of Nonconformists is not precisely identical with that of the Presbyterian churches, with which Anglicans in the past owned fraternity; and, within England and Wales, there are legal obstacles to intercommunion which we may regret, but cannot ignore. These obstacles, however, do not exist in the Mission field, and there the question resolves itself into this crucial point, What principles shall determine our relations with non-Anglicans? Are we to proceed on the principles of Anglicanism, as these were generally understood from Cranmer to Newman, or are we to give formal and final endorsement to the Tractarian repudiation of those principles, and acquiesce in an isolation, sterilizing and complete, alike from the older episcopal Churches which were never reformed, and from the newer non-episcopal Churches which share with ourselves the heritage of the Reformation?

H. Hensley Henson, *Retrospect of an Unimportant Life* (3 vols, 1942–50), I, 162.

12 Conclusion

When Cosmo Gordon Lang, Archbishop of Canterbury from 1928 to 1942, was looking back on his life, he wrote:

> I have always considered that the years—say 1890 to 1914—were the Golden Age of parochial work in the towns of England. In spite of all controversies—the growing pains of the Church—the ideals of the long and steady Church Revival had taken hold. What may be called 'the social consciousness' of the Church had been roused by Maurice and Kingsley and more recently by men like Gore and Scott Holland. The work of the Church had grown in the intensity of faith and worship and in the extent of its range. There were able and devoted men in charge of industrial parishes everywhere; and the public schools and universities and theological colleges were still sending out full supplies of keen and healthy young men to help them ... My memory is of a Church life humming with activity and hopeful persistence in its task.
>
> J. G. Lockhart, *Cosmo Gordon Lang* (1949), 155–6.

Outwardly, too, the Nonconformists in England still seemed to be flourishing. The old generation of their preachers had passed, but they had their successors who still drew large congregations. At the great Congregationalist stronghold, the City Temple in London, Joseph Parker (1830–1902), who had preached there for over thirty years, had been succeeded by the young, brilliant, controversial Reginald John Campbell. He was, unlike Parker, a theological liberal with a 'New Theology' which he expounded in a persuasive and scholarly way; and each Thursday at noon thousands heard for sixty minutes this handsome, silver-voiced preacher. A report in the *Daily Telegraph* in 1903 described the scene:

> There were thousands of us in the pews at the City Temple yesternoon, and one man was in the pulpit. We had come from warehouses and offices, from banks and shops, from the Exchange and the markets, giving up our dinner-hour, and taking our snack of food when or where or how we could, so that a higher

purpose was duly served. And what had we come out for to hear? Simply Carlyle's 'Speaking Man'.

Daily Telegraph, 1903. Quoted, Leonard Griffiths, *Barriers to Christian Belief* (1962), 11.

A legacy from the nineteenth century—Fourah Bay College, Sierra Leone, built from the timber of captured slave-ships

Yet it was already clear that the new century was bringing serious problems for religion in England. This was realized in 1913 by Cyril Garbett, who was then Vicar of Portsea and was to be Archbishop of York from 1942 to 1955. In that year he organized a carefully prepared parochial mission, which he strongly felt was a failure because its influence had made itself felt more among the churchgoers than among those utterly indifferent. Some forty years later in a Visitation Charge as Archbishop of York, he said:

It is comparatively easy to know the good news the Church should give; it is much harder to know how to get it across. Waste of effort and disappointment are caused by frequent failure to see that *evangelistic methods once successful are now too often ineffective.*

Charles Smyth, *Cyril Forster Garbett* (1959), 127.

And while clergymen in leading positions in the Church of England were experiencing illuminating disappointments, the Nonconformists were making discoveries that were at least as disconcerting. They had sought to maintain an aloofness from the ordinary pursuits and pleasures of everyday life, but now many of them were becoming unwilling to do this. In an address on 'The Secularisation of the Church', the Chairman of the Congregational Union in 1894 said:

Christian parents no longer forbid their children to read novels or to learn dancing; some of them accompany their sons and daughters to the theatre and the concert; in many Christian homes billiards and cards are allowed, and both in occupation and amusement the line that once divided the world from the Church is tending to disappear.

G. S. Barrett, in *Congregational Year Book* (1895), 47.

The Salvation Army, which many had hoped would achieve more success than others, was becoming more and more an agency for social work among the poor and finding that its evangelistic methods were hardly more successful than the parochial missions of the Church. An intelligent American, Robert Woods, who was surveying English religious movements in the 1890s, wrote:

It ought to be well understood that before the Salvation Army took up definite social work it had little, if any, more success than other evangelistic agencies have among these people. The campaign of purely emotional religion in the East End of London was a failure.

R. A. Woods, *English Social Movements* (2nd ed, 1895), 170.

Behind these signs of the difficulties experienced by organized religion in maintaining its position and its failure to spread its message were many factors. One was a growing neglect of the Bible which Matthew Arnold spoke about as early as 1873. By its literal stress on the Bible, Evangelicalism had made the English the 'people of a book' in a way unknown in other countries, but now people were reading it less and respecting it less. This was so widespread that it was probably due to more than one reason, though Matthew Arnold connected it with the doubts about the veracity and relevance of the Bible:

> But now it is *the people* which is getting detached from the Bible. The masses can no longer be relied on to counteract what the cultivated wits are doing, and stubbornly to make clever men's extravagances and aberrations, if about the Bible they commit them, of no avail. When our philosophical Liberal friends say, that by universal suffrage, public meetings, Church-disestablishment, marrying one's deceased wife's sister, secular schools, industrial development, man can live very well; and that if he studies the writings, say, of Mr Herbert Spencer into the bargain, he will be perfect, he 'will have in modern and congenial language the truisms common to all systems of morality', and the Bible is become quite old-fashioned and superfluous for him;—when our philosophical friends now say this, the masses, far from checking them, are disposed to applaud them to the echo. Yet assuredly, of conduct, which is more than three-fourths of human life, the Bible, whatever people may thus think and say, is the great inspirer; so that from the great inspirer of more than three-fourths of human life the masses of our society now seem to be cutting themselves off. This promises, certainly, if it does not already constitute, a very unsettled condition of things. And the cause of it lies in the Bible being made to depend on a story, or set of asserted facts, which it is impossible to verify; and which hard-headed people, therefore, treat as either an imposture, or a fairy-tale that discredits all that is found in connexion with it.

Matthew Arnold, *Literature and Dogma* (1873), chap x.

Another factor was the declining place of dogma in Protestantism in general and in Nonconformity in particular. The coherent 'plan of salvation', inherited from Calvinism, which had been erected into such an imposing structure of faith, was now being sapped at its very foundations. This also was discerned by Matthew Arnold when, in his old age, he wrote this passage in 1886 as part of the Preface to a popular edition of his *St Paul and Protestantism*:

> Time moves and Opinion moves with it; moves to-day, how fast, how sweepingly! I turn over the pages of *St Paul and Protestantism*, written some sixteen years ago; what has become of the doctrines of unscriptural Protestantism criticised in it? Sixteen years ago the movement of time and change had indeed

reached them, even in this country. But now it has so prevailed over them that the careful exhibition and criticism of them, in the pages which follow, seems almost a waste of labour. Where are now those great and grave doctrines which so possessed the thoughts of religious England formerly? Where is the doctrine of predestination?—gone! Where are the doctrines of original sin, imputed righteousness, and justification by faith? where are they, not as tenets to be formally professed, but as doctrines to fill and form man's mind and soul? They are fast going. Where, too, is the 'Dissidence of Dissent', with its 'spirit of watchful jealousy'? The Liberals of the nadir still hope to conjure with it; but what open mind does not now perceive its narrowness, poverty, and sterility?

Matthew Arnold, *St Paul and Protestantism* (1886), Preface.

Another central feature of Protestantism had long been the sermon, the exposition of the Word of God. Although people still crowded to hear popular preachers, it was also apparent that the sermon was losing its power in later nineteenth-century England, and that this was happening among all classes of the people. The spread of education and of cheap literature was destroying the place it once held as the sole purveyor of interest and information among the masses, but perhaps even more serious, as was pointed out in an article in *The Nineteenth Century* in 1877, was its failure to hold the respect of the educated classes:

There is the rapidly growing intellectual class, which we are told is coming to regard the preacher and his unverifiable assertions with quiet indifference or scorn; and it is confidently predicted that, as culture advances, the pulpit, the whole system of things in which it is a power, will be left behind among the worn-out superstitions of mankind. There can be no doubt that there is a peculiar virulence in the tone of some of the doctors of the school which has now justly the ear of the public towards the preacher and his thoughts and ways. And hence arises a truly formidable danger. But I hold that for this antagonism the pulpit is mainly responsible. It is reaping as it has sown, and it has to pass through its time of humiliation. The preacher readily entertains the notion that the whole scheme of things is laid out to his small understanding in the word of God. He seems as if he came down on the vast range of subjects which he is tempted to handle as from a superior height; and this is what the scientific mind can never endure. The place of theology in the sphere of man's knowledge tempts its doctors to believe that it confers the right of speaking with a certain decision on all kinds of topics; and there has always been a sort of omniscient tone in the pulpit method of handling intellectual questions which stirs fierce rebellion in cultivated minds and hearts.

J. Baldwin Brown, 'Is the Pulpit Losing its Power?', *The Nineteenth Century* (March 1877), in Michael Goodwin (ed), *Nineteenth-Century Opinion* (1951), 127.

Charles Darwin

Of the scientific developments of the time, that most hostile to contemporary religion was the theory of evolution put forward by Charles Darwin (1809–92) in his book, *The Origin of Species by Means of Natural Selection*, which was published in 1859. Darwin himself made it clear that he had no desire to weaken the authority of religion, and in the Conclusion to the book he sought to reconcile a religious and a scientific view of the universe:

> Thus, from the war of nature, from famine and death, the most exalted object of which we are capable of conceiving, namely, the production of the higher animals, directly follows. There is grandeur in this view of life, with its several powers, having been originally breathed by the Creator into a few forms, or into one; and that, whilst this planet has gone cycling on according to the fixed law of gravity, from so simple a beginning endless forms most beautiful and most wonderful have been, and are being, evolved.
>
> Quoted, William Irvine, *Apes, Angels and Victorians* (1956), 75.

There were scientists, however, who were not prepared to accept Darwin's view. The most prominent of these was Thomas Henry Huxley (1825–95), who described himself as acting as 'Darwin's bulldog' and introduced the term agnosticism in 1869 to represent the doctrine that man does not know and cannot know anything about the existence of a God or anything beyond material phenomena. Twenty years later he developed his position in an article by asking a series of questions about Jesus:

> In the course of other inquiries, I have had to do with fossil remains which looked quite plain at a distance and became more and more indistinct as I tried to define their outline by close inspection. There was something there—something which, if I could win assurance about it, might mark a new epoch in the history of the earth; but, study as I might, certainty eluded my grasp. So it has been with me in my efforts to define the grand figure of Jesus as it lies in the primary strata of Christian literature. Is he the kindly, peaceful Christ depicted in the Catacombs? Or is he the stern judge who frowns above the altar of SS Cosmas and Damianus? Or can he be rightly represented in the bleeding ascetic, broken down by physical pain, of too many medieval pictures? Are we to accept the Jesus of the second, or the Jesus of the fourth gospel, as the true Jesus? What did he really say and do; and how much that is attributed to him in speech and action is the embroidery of the various parties into which his followers tended to split themselves within twenty years of his death, when even the threefold tradition was only nascent?
>
> T. H. Huxley, 'Agnosticism', *The Nineteenth Century* (February 1889), in M. Goodwin, *op cit*, 120.

That Huxley could write thus revealed the general ignorance in England of the trends of Biblical study which had been proceeding elsewhere, particularly in Germany, for some time. And, indeed, if English organized religion had not been bound by its view of the verbal inspiration of the Bible, which prevented it listening calmly to anyone who denied the historicity of the Book of Genesis or questioned the actuality of the miracles of the New Testament, it would not have had anything to fear from his onslaughts which he pressed with religious fervour; but, as it was, he was presented with an easy target, and his numerous articles, such as 'Science and the Bishops' written in 1887, convinced many people that Christianity and the new scientific knowledge were inevitably opposed:

> I do not know any body of scientific men who could be got to listen without the strongest expressions of disgusted repudiation to the exposition of a pretended scientific discovery, which had no better evidence to show for itself than the story of the devils entering a herd of swine, or of the fig-tree that was blasted for bearing no figs when 'it was not the season of figs'. Whether such events are possible or impossible, no man can say; but scientific ethics can and does declare that the profession of belief in them, on the evidence of documents of unknown date and of unknown authorship, is immoral. Theological apologists who insist that morality will vanish if their dogmas are exploded, would do well to consider the fact that, in the matter of intellectual veracity, science is already a long way ahead of the Churches; and that, in this particular, it is exerting an educational influence on mankind of which the Churches have shown themselves utterly incapable.
>
> T. H. Huxley, 'Science and the Bishops', *The Nineteenth Century* (November 1887), *ibid*, 146.

Huxley's arguments may seem shallow, but they were symptomatic of a great change that was slowly but inexorably (though hardly realized at the time) taking place in the attitude of public opinion towards the Christian religion. Reflecting upon this period, Beatrice Webb wrote in her autobiography:

> For, looking back, it now seems to me that it was exactly in those last decades of the nineteenth century that we find the watershed between the metaphysic of the Christian Church, which had hitherto dominated British civilisation, and the agnosticism, deeply coloured by scientific materialism, which was destined, during the first decades of the twentieth century, to submerge all religion based on tradition and revelation. Judging by my own experience among the organisers of big enterprise, with their 'business morality' and their international affiliations, the Christian tradition, already in the 'seventies and 'eighties, had grown thin and brittle, more easily broken than repaired.
>
> Beatrice Webb, *My Apprenticeship* (Penguin ed, 2 vols, 1938, I, 73–4).

The consequences of such a situation were at first also incompletely apprehended, especially in religious circles. Much truth, however, was contained in C. F. G. Masterman's prophetic diagnosis of the religious situation, which was written in the first decade of the twentieth century:

> ... Belief in religion, as a conception of life dependent upon supernatural sanctions or as a revelation of a purpose and meaning beyond the actual business of the day, is slowly but steadily fading from the modern city race....
>
> ... The drift is towards a non-dogmatic affirmation of general kindliness and good fellowship, with an emphasis rather on the service of men than the fulfilment of the Will of God.... Ethical advance is accompanied (as it seems) by spiritual decline. It was the process which so perplexed Mr Gladstone more than half a century ago.... The work of civilisation steadily advances. The vision of a universe beyond or behind the material steadily fades.
>
> C. F. G. Masterman, *The Condition of England* (1909), ch IX ('Religion and Progress').

As they began to apprehend the situation, the reaction of Christian writers to the new developments was critical, and they soon raised issues which still remain unanswered in our own time. Thus, R. W. Church, writing in 1877 asserted that ethical standards could not exist in isolation, but only in conjunction with the Christian religion with which it had been historically associated:

> It is a matter of history that in what we now generally accept as true morality there are two factors: (1) On the one hand, human experience, human reasonableness, human good feeling, human self-restraint; and (2) on the other, the belief, the laws, the ideas, the power of Christianity. It is difficult to conceive what reason there is to expect that if one factor is taken away the result will continue the same: that the removal or weakening of such an important one as Christianity would not seriously affect such departments of morals as purity, the relations of the strong to the weak, respect for human life, slavery.
>
> R. W. Church, 'A Modern Symposium—4', *The Nineteenth Century* (April 1877), in M. Goodwin, *op cit*, 138.

And John Neville Figgis (1866–1919), a historian and theologian of unusual brilliance and depth of thought, ended the second of his Hulsean Lectures, delivered in 1908, with moving words about the nature of the reduced Christianity which he saw as the consequence of the decline of dogmatic theology:

Take from the Christian faith its mystery and strangeness, and see what is left. Is the creed when 'trimmed and stripped of all that touches the skies' a beautiful or even a helpful thing? . . . Leave out, if you must, the mysterious birth, the availing death, the empty tomb, and the sacramental presence, and what would you have left? Would it be very much to live by? Would it be anything at all to die for?

Quoted, L. E. Elliott-Binns, *The Development of English Theology in the Later Nineteenth Century* (1952), 112.

Glossary

APOSTOLIC SUCCESSION. The method by which the ministry of the Church is held to be derived in a continuous succession from the apostles to the bishops by the laying on of hands.

BAPTISMAL REGENERATION. The spiritual rebirth, bringing about a change from a sensual to a Christian life, which, according to traditional Christian belief, is effected in the soul by baptism.

CANON. A clergyman attached to a cathedral and observing its rule or canon.

CHALCEDON, COUNCIL OF (A.D. 451). A Council of the Church which met to deal with the Eutychian* heresy and drew up a manifesto of faith which was accepted by the Catholic Church.

CHAPTER. The body of persons concerned with the management of an institution, especially the canons* of a cathedral.

CHURCH RATES. A compulsory levy made upon parishioners to keep the parish church in repair, which was abolished in 1868.

CONVOCATIONS. The Convocations of Canterbury and York, the ancient assemblies of the Church of England, each divided into two houses—the upper, consisting of bishops, and the lower, made up of deans, canons, archdeacons and proctors (elected representatives of the lower clergy).

CORPORATION ACT (1661) required all municipal office holders to take Communion according to the Church of England. From 1727 Annual Indemnity Acts were passed to protect those who disregarded its requirement, and it was repealed in 1828.

DEAN. The head of the clergy attached to a cathedral.

DEPRIVATION. The deposition of a clergyman from his position in the Church.

DONATISTS. A sect which arose in the Christian Church in North Africa at the beginning of the fourth century and became separated from the Catholic Church. The spread of their numbers soon brought about rival bishops throughout North Africa. The Donatists excommunicated the rest of the Church, baptizing again all Catholics who seceded to them. They persisted until the African Church was destroyed by the Saracens in the seventh century.

EPISCOPALLY ORDAINED. Admitted to the Christian ministry by the laying on of hands by a bishop as required by belief in the apostolic succession.*

EUTYCHIANS. The followers of Eutyches (c. 378–454), whose views about the person of Christ were condemned by the Council of Chalcedon.*

FORMULARIES. Statements of belief, particularly, for the Church of England, the Book of Common Prayer and the Thirty-nine Articles.

LAMBETH CONFERENCE. The assembly of the bishops of the whole Anglican communion, which has been held about every ten years since 1867 at Lambeth Palace under the presidency of the Archbishop of Canterbury.

MINOR CANON. A clergyman attached to a cathedral to assist in the singing of the daily service.

MONOPHYSITES. Those who rejected the manifesto of faith of the Council of Chalcedon* and held that Christ had only one composite nature instead of the orthodox doctrine that He united two complete natures, human and divine, in one person.

NEOPLATONISM. A system of philosophy combining Platonic and Oriental elements originating at Alexandria in the third century.

NON-RESIDENCE. The failure of a clergyman to reside in the place in which he is authorized to minister.

ORDINATION. The act of admission to the Christian ministry. One who is to be ordained is known as an ordinand.

PLURALISM. The holding by a clergyman of more than one office in the Church, which is made possible by non-residence.*

REAL PRESENCE. The belief in the actual presence in the consecrated bread and wine in the Eucharist of the Body and Blood of Christ, as opposed to the ideas of those who maintain that the Body and Blood are present only symbolically or figuratively.

RESERVATION. The practice of keeping part of the consecrated bread (and sometimes also the wine) of the Eucharist, primarily for the communion of the sick.

RESIDENTIARY. The name for a canon* of a cathedral, who is bound to reside there for a certain time every year.

SACRIFICE. An offering made to God with a view to communion with Him, for His honour and for the benefit of souls, especially in the Eucharist as a representation of the sacrificial death of Christ for mankind.

SINECURE. A salaried post without duties attached, especially an ecclesiastical office without the care or cure of souls.

STIPEND. A fixed periodical money payment, especially to a clergyman.

TEST ACT (1673) required all holders of civil and military posts to take Communion according to the Church of England. It was repealed in 1828.

TRENT, COUNCIL OF (1545–63). A Council of the Roman Catholic Church, which settled the doctrines of the Church in opposition to those of the Reformation, reformed its discipline and strengthened the authority of the Pope.

TRIDENTINE. Pertaining to the Council of Trent or to its decrees.

Books for Further Reading

The best general book for this period is O. Chadwick, *The Victorian Church* (2 vols, 1966–70). On the Church of England there is S. C. Carpenter, *Church and People 1789–1889* (1933) and for the last part of the period, R. Lloyd, *The Church of England 1900–65* (1966). For Nonconformity there is E. A. Payne, *The Free Church Tradition in the Life of England* (1965), and M. Edwards, *Methodism and England* (1943), and for Roman Catholicism, E. I. Watkin, *Roman Catholicism in England to 1950* (1957).

The Evangelical movement is well described in E. M. Howse, *Saints in Politics: The Clapham Sect and the Growth of Freedom* (1952), and C. H. E. Smyth, *Simeon and Church Order* (1940); the Tractarians in Y. Brilioth, *The Anglican Revival* (1925), and G. Faber, *Oxford Apostles* (1933); and a general consideration of the Anglican controversies is to be found in A. O. J. Cockshut, *Anglican Attitudes* (1959). Biographies include J. Coupland, *Wilberforce* (2nd ed, 1945), M. Trevor, *John Henry Newman* (2 vols, 1962) and Florence Higham, *Frederick Denison Maurice* (1947).

For religious ideas the best general survey is L. E. Elliott-Binns, *Religion in the Victorian Era* (1936), to which may be added V. F. Storr, *The Development of English Theology in the Nineteenth Century 1800–60* (1913) and L. E. Elliott-Binns, *English Thought 1860–1900: the Theological Aspect* (1956).

The later part of the period is richly served by ecclesiastical biographies, two excellent examples being R. T. Davidson and W. Benham, *Archibald Campbell Tait, Archbishop of Canterbury* (2 vols, 1891), and *The Life and Letters of Mandell Creighton, Bishop of London*, by his wife (2 vols, 1904). There is also E. S. Purcell, *Life of Cardinal Manning* (1896). (Only the first edition is of value.)

Index

9781138084346